Praise

George Wallace – winner
Festival ÓRPHEUS – PLOVDIV 2018 with his poem
'Orpheus on the Ebros' — is one of the best contemporary
world's poets I have ever read. His poetry is like a message
from God, but it isn't enough to say that because while
plenty of poets think that they write under God's dictation,
to hear the message, to catch the message, is different. In its
energy, a sliver of the Beats (A hundred years among the
daisies). In its reflectiveness, a particle of the Postmodernists
(Letters from Vincent). But the essence of this strong
masculine poetry is the Message — the message to the people,
the message to the future, like a man who dies twice does not
die / at all, he is Lazarus, he comes back to life, reborn. This is
a poetry written in the language of the Prophets. This is a
poetry with contempt for the floods of the world — the seas
and rivers, time and memory, history and the future — in
their present tense. The real message of this poetry is its
attempt to unite a divided world.

—Anton Baev, poet, writer, Chairman,
Plovdiv Writers' Union

A vast collection of delightful and bewildering wisdom,
poems that expand and explode upon the paper,
each petal of a mountainside of daisies, tattooed with
exquisiteness. I highly recommend this book.

—Catfish McDaris, postal worker,
Thelonious Monk Award

Like Whitman, Wallace has the uncanny ability to absorb the world around him and become one with it. But perhaps what is most profound about Wallace's voice is the passion that radiates through his images and infuses us with a yearning to join him, an all-encompassing love for life despite, as well as because of, all of its disparities.

—Olga Abella, Editor, *Bluestem*

Octavio Paz in his Nobel address said poetry will save the world. George Wallace has attended this point & made it the premise of his art.

—Allen Planz, sea captain, NEA fellow

One Hundred Years Among the Daisies

Poems by
George Wallace

Stubborn Mule Press
Devil's Elbow, MO
stubbornmulepress.com

Copyright (c) George Wallace, 2018
First Edition 1 3 5 7 9 10 8 6 4 2
ISBN: 978-1-946642-68-4
LCCN: 2018955397

Design, edits and layout: Jeanette Powers
Cover image: Jon Lee Grafton
Author photos: Shell Sheddy, Charlotte Mann
All rights reserved. No part of this publication may be reproduced or transmitted in any form or by any means, electronic or mechanical, including photocopying, recording or by info retrieval system, without prior written permission from the author.

Some of the poems in this manuscript have appeared individually in: *Beat Laureate Anthology (If you could remove the dead from the dead, If rocks were huckleberries and every oak leaf a message from god; how the mist moves); Begin Again, 150 Kansas Poems (The dancing cottage; The road leads north across the desert); BigCityLit (I will take the steep boat down; Good morning rainbird with ocean in your wings; This shadow like blood before my eyes; I take the mystic blue taxi to you); Cave Moon Press, Pazarte (He remembers the sun, the only light he sees; For this my heart, the revolution); Home Planet News (Emenescu's Waves, The Olive Pickers, In The Shadow of Dreamtown, Dawn breaks over the Black Sea); Orpheus Festival Anthology (Trapped in amber, fatal to the touch; Orpheus floating down the Ebros; Wax wings, feather wings); Poets Responding (How it will End, No Golden Fleece will save you, saviors); Portrete de frontier (An army of men to keep men out); Ramingo's Porch (Cell door Opening, Cendrar's Monkey); Waymark (100 years among the daisies; Easy; To take you up whole, to drink you up whole; I open my eyes; In your hermitage of work or sleep; Rain skip a stone on me).*

The poetry sequence *Letters From Vincent (Poems, Constructions, Collages and Intertextual Improvisations drawn from the letters of Vincent Van Gogh)* appeared in the anthology *Resurrections of a Sunflower,* published by Pski's Porch in 2017.

CONTENTS

One Hundred Years Among the Poems / by John Dorsey
One hundred years among the daisies / 1
Dawn breaks over the Black Sea / 2
A hillside on the slopes of Parnassus / 4
Rain skip a stone on me / 6
Wax wings, feather wings / 7
Orpheus on the Ebros / 8
I will take the steep boat down / 9
The dancing cottage / 10
If you could remove the dead from the dead / 12
How it will end / 14
Of time honor and memory / 16
The road leads north across the desert / 17
Visions signs and bagatelles / 19
America the beautiful / 21
Climbing Mount Diablo / 22
Chrysler building in snow / 24
Walking Cordelia / 25
How the mist moves / 26
If rocks were huckleberries and every oak leaf a message
  from god / 27
To come devoted into the arms of love / 28
In your hermitage of work or sleep / 30
To harp down day with its blooded neck / 32
Love folds deep into the fold / 33
To take you up whole, to drink you up whole / 35
The crease in his smile that ran straight through her heart / 36
Harmonizing with the crickets / 38
The lyrical spike has landed / 39

Dream child illuminates herself / 40
Pull an angel from the flesh of man / 41
Yo soy mecapalli / 43
One green acre of summer corn / 46
Black ant on the countertop, two deer in a yellow field / 48
Lone Star lollipop / 50
Gyorgy Kastriotis / 53
Eighth Day rising / 55
No not the Vardar / 56
The heart is a good soldier it keeps on ticking / 58
Ass forward thru oceans / 60
The fellaheen who saunter through open markets / 64
A shadow which has been following us a very long time / 65
Grazing like cattle between speckled grass and sky / 67
Cendrar's monkey / 69
One earth one people / 71
Watch me burn it to the ground in the tallgrass, baby / 74
Lavendar Tee and dogtag chain / 76
You and me dad / 78
Good morning rainbird with ocean in your wings / 80
This shadow like blood before my eyes / 83
I take the mystic blue taxi to you / 85
A Persian Rose / 87
The Olive Pickers / 89
Standing by a Palladian window sweating over piano keys / 90
Every embrace a cloud, every kiss fresh as fresh water / 92
Letters from Vincent:
  A fatal marriage with the sea / 94
  Landscape with decaying oak trunks / 95

Café terrace at night / 96

Roulen the Postman / 97

A synthesis of Arlesiennes / 98

Red herrings / 100

A commune in the Bouche de Rhone / 102

Illuminations and fireworks postponed
  for stormy weateher / 104

Terribly alone, forever young / 106

Missing portrait / 108

In life his life was beautiful / 109

Sunset, Easter sunset / 111

We are bigger than flowers / 112

Easy / 113

Not the kissing kind / 114

I could never explain / 115

An army of men to keep men out / 116

Trapped in amber, fatal to the touch / 118

Given without reserve, taken to life's limit / 119

A rainy afternoon in New York City / 120

Shadow of dreamtown / 122

The blind emptiness of hands / 124

No Golden Fleece will save you, saviors / 126

Provenance / 128

He remembers the sun, the only light he sees / 130

I open my eyes / 131

Cell door opening / 133

Watchful as the wild / 135

Emenescu's Waves / 136

For this my heart, the revolution / 138

One Hundred Years Among the Poems

Well, maybe not a full century, but my friend George Wallace has been at this a long time. He has almost become an institution, but that tends to happen when you have devoted a lifetime to anything, and to poetry in particular. It's not an easy life and not an easy thing to do most days. I don't care what the the title poem of this collection says, George is far from a simple man, he is giving, generous and as complicated as anyone who stretches lines out of thin air usually is. One thing in those opening lines is true, he is an alleycat, someone who is starving for beauty, & someone who feeds his soul wherever he can find it.

I first came across George and his work during the early days of my friendship with S.A. Griffin and the late great Scott Wannberg, and thought immediately that George had the heart of jazz poet, like Howard Hart or Ray Bremser before him, & the soul of someone who was searching for something bigger. I think I was right on both counts.

This recent collection though feels like something else entirely, well maybe not entirely, but it feels like it comes from the Earth, it is an organic bebop, one man's history with the world and those who inhabit his time & space. I don't think George could've written a book like this when he was first getting started or even when he & I first met. That isn't a slight, but a glowing compliment, a testament to the fact that the great ones never stop growing, like daisies themselves, their words always seem to spring up again with new life & George seems to me to be at his peak here, dense & organic, wild & free, take from these poems what you will, because they offer everything, but just leave George to his jukebox, because it feels like wisdom, it feels like truth, it feels like home.

I know most scholars might offer you pieces of the poems inside, giving examples of what they are supposed to mean, but like George himself, they can offer so much to so many & I would never dare try to box them in. So I will just say, keep reading beyond this page, George is way more interesting than I am, I'm just blessed to have him in my life, to call him my friend & now with this book, you're blessed to, you have his poems.

This book isn't dedicated to one path, but it will always lead you in the right direction, all you have to do is turn the page & keep moving forward.

—John Dorsey, Poet Laureate
of Belle, Missouri, 9-9-18

One Hundred Years
Among the Daisies

ONE HUNDRED YEARS AMONG THE DAISIES

I am a simple man an alleycat I do not travel
far or well and i do not believe in miracles,
i was born in this place i do not test well for
generosity or your ordinary measures of
success; push me I will push back, leave me
to my jukebox and my beer and we will get
along just fine; yes I was born here, a harbor
town, we call it fish heads and valentines,
I'm simple as rope, a bait and tackle kind
of guy, my hull chafes the dock at dawn,
my engine churns oily waters — at night
when I dream, a gull flies among eagles
and if it rains so what, I soak rain up like
pickle brine, I drink it down and call it
champagne. do wharf rats run with their
own well so do I — are you so very different
with your earrings or your college degrees?
when midnight comes who owns the stars?
the wind blows equally on all men, and the
waves belong to the man who will sail out into
them. I know I lack humor but I also know what
I lack; the shape of my face in the mirror is my own
face and I know what's what at closing time. show me
the exit sign I'll be on my way. show me a good time
and it's go cat go because time is bodies in motion
and I am a patient man and a man of action – throw
me like a brick over a garden wall and I will lie there
among the daisies a hundred years, if necessary,
a hundred years — but I will find my mate.

DAWN BREAKS OVER THE BLACK SEA

One of several small children is hidden among deck chairs, his eyes reflect the sea, more coral than green, and the sea is irked, the black sea is glaring, and he is irked, this small boy, as the adults pass, as the adults take their long rolling strides and greet the dawn, as they greet each other, predictably in the weak predictable light, and his mother is one of them, and the black sea does its business without reflection, like a nation in the grip of war, like a large city releasing dark birds back into the sky, the Black Sea, which is eternal, and this passage which is meant to be an enlarged form of their world, something eternal and much larger than what happens back home, in their lives, in their successes and disappointments, in their dreams and desires

And dawn wraps itself up and spits itself out on the deck of the ship, in itself redundant and eternal and small, like a champagne cork on a rolling deck, and dawn breaks and breaks — many people are breaking just now in this world, which is at war with itself — and she is one of them, the mother of one of several small children hidden among the deck chairs, she is breaking, and what can adults say that will allow them to escape or to hide? something in this atmosphere escapes the adults, only children can feel it, a grievance in the salt and mist, a revolt in the horizon, a truth, a truth, only children can feel it, and anyhow the mother of the boy is distracted, she was pretty in Vienna where the light was artificial and gay, she bends her neck to greet the gaze of the men who pass her

But it is not the same, she turns to the man with whom she is walking and says something private and hideous and true, and his eyes sparkle and he looks away, and his eyes are clear as the rays of the rising sun

A HILLSIDE IN THE SLOPES OF PARNASSUS

Quick moving, nimble,
eating oleander, I can
see you from here, with
my Mountain Goat eyes,
feel you from here, with my
Mountain Goat limbs, I can
taste you from here, decipher
your DNA, with my crazy mouth,
and my crooked eyes blinding;
and my hot tongue wagging,
blind as an idiot in a cave,
listening for voices, eyes
open wide before the
mystic oracle,
no need of sight
inside the Cave of Man
he who sees, sees with his hands,
inhaling the earth,
I inhale you, snake vapors!
you grow in my belly
like giant diamonds,
like venom like pearls,
you come to me out of
the dark place and press
your lips to my mouth,
Om to the black sapphire,
and to the enormous pit of emptiness,
and Coretas the Shepherd Boy
has got nothing on me, neither

shall the Thessalonian avail,
and I will eat the leaves of oleander
and be one with you in the sweet dark
emptiness, and the almond grove at dusk,
sweet night come, sweet sweet night,
and your breath in my hair —
incorrect, dangerous, horny,
near — and the night air cool,
and I, climbing like jasmine, a vine,
and you the garden on the hill
hanging by a thread to this loom
of language, hanging on prophecy
which would bind us, O garden,
O love, woven by no man,
Time is time and time is nothing,
Distance nothing, beyond the
blossoming of a flower

and I, like a crazy goat
  am eating
oleander
  on a hillside
in the slopes of
  Parnassus

RAIN SKIP A STONE ON ME

I am a lake I live on this planet I love the way this planet rolls it gets me high, I travel the world faithfully, I stay where I am, here is where I belong, in one place, in one piece, I see the future, the future is me, heaven rotates thru my belly, when lovers walk along my shore they honor me and take me with them, when small boys catch my fish with their fishing line it tickles my belly it gets me high. Do things change for you? I remain the same. This is how I do things, 30 million years,

Do you like this, can you dig this, this is how we do this thing, like then like now, live like a swan, live like a fish, like a snail like a minnow like muck, and I am straight as whiskey and whiskey loves a duck, and a small bank of clouds on the blue horizon is my best friend, that's where the sun comes from and also rain and the tribes of men, and rain is snow and snow feeds the mountains and the mountains feed me, they fill up with women and men and they empty out,

And the mountains feed the streams and the streams feed me, therefore the mountains and the streams are my best friend and people come and people go, and every day I love you more — more than wind rain and heaven and stone.

So stoned! Rain skip a stone on me.

WAX WINGS, FEATHER WINGS

I listen to the Mediterranean roll, the sea at night with blue dolphins in it, I sleep inside a cave in Mykonos, I listen at the mouth of every cave, that one in Patmos, that's where i heard the voice of the Titans, Titans! Laughing and tossing sixteen sided dice

Words and prophecies are dice tossed at heaven, the Titans are a crowd of big-time gamblers and noisy as waterfalls, and I don't mind

And dice rattle in mountaintops like the green breath of a Zephyr wind, they bound among the stars, like spring lambs, they cry like shepherd boys and sing like goldfinches as they tumble along, sweet little seeds tossed by Titans, like wings, like luck

Wings, wings and prophecies — sometimes words fail me, and who trusts the gods around here, give me wings, wax wings, feather wings, wings of goldfinches and the hands of clocks and hummingbirds, wings of dice tossed by Titans that have no other reason to exist than to damn gravity and experience the joy of flight

ORPHEUS ON THE EBROS

Words are made of air and it is to air that they will return
                —Trevor Dadson

And still it comes to this, my head floating downriver, daring to take in air and let it out again, not in the shape of the hearts of women or men, women and women and young men dancing, but in the shape of loss and the lyre in song, mystery of the gods to give presence to the world where presence is absent,

To sing the pastures and the fields that pass me as I go, silent fields of Thrace, Maenaeds with their stones and bare hands, in the cold light of the glade, to calm down nature and tame what is wild, air and tree, give voice to the silent creatures of pasture and forest, to take their grief and give it back as praise,

Before the first snow comes, I mean, before my body is gone forever, before there is nothing left of me but voice, voice to sing away absence, I in my turn taken in, like air, and given back to the world freely, imperfect son of the earth whose song is grief, whose love is Eurydice, the fecundity of earth, how quickly

It passes, seasons and sufficiencies, beauty of song, the limits of power given us by the gods, and all taken back by them, as I pass by on my way to the sea.

I WILL TAKE THE STEEP BOAT DOWN

I will take the steep boat down, downriver to where the swans glide and the deep pools eddy, to where sunlight rides in easy circles like magic or motorcycles, to a place where the replenishment of soil and the turbulence of seed, and a cantata of calm eases the heart

I will dance across simple waters, like an insect sacred unto itself, deferential as a woodland flower, fresh as acknowledgement of simple desire, and dancing on liquid surfaces I shall take the long ride, forgetting my French lessons, forgetting geography and mathematics and the law

And flee like the river, down to the place where no rivers go, to the place where rainbow trout, shimmering with their siblings, like raindrops, display their liquid scales golden against the light, and the clear water slow and dark, and the riverbird with his black beak which swoops and sails

For the fulfillment of love, with respect for everything, for the sake of simple disembarkation, I will go there, alone along the riverbank and wooded path, in full immersion, drink down the sun after rain and go like beauty goes, and stay like beauty stays, a blackberry ripening in the thicket, an oakleaf quivering like a piccolo as it falls,

And walk with the angel of forgetfulness, which shades men's hearts and delivers them from the verge of pain

THE DANCING COTTAGE

Before she came to America your grandmother served three sisters in a cottage in Russia, a dancing cottage that turned and turned among the trees, a woodcutter's cottage in a clearing in a forest and the woodcutter was never home, a modest cottage, a chickenlegged cottage that turned and turned with three ugly sisters inside,

Woodsman's daughters they were and your grandmother was servant to the three of them and she was small and capable, and silent and quick, when she plucked a chicken she was a fistful of feathers and the woodcutter was never home, and the three sisters laughed at your grandmother, her clothes and her smell and her manners,

She belonged outside where she was born they said, she smelled like the skin of animals — and the truth of the matter is your grandmother DID spring out of the earth, like a mushroom, near a tree where the cottage pigs dug up roots in summer, and when she walked through the cottage a chill like outdoors followed her from room to room,

And the three sisters were afraid of that and they didn't like the look in her eyes and called her Baba, as in Baba Yaga, they called her that right in front of her face, and she said nothing and tended the smoky stove and cleaned things up, and she could push the handle of a broom straight through straw to chase away mice if it was necessary,

And in the candlelight of evening the cottage danced
and the pine forest was silent and watchful, and the silence
was terrible and wonderful and enchanted at the same time,
and the clatter of chicken bones and metal plates, and in
winter the three sisters ate turnip soup and
laughed and were very happy,

And the woodsman was not there, and the wind shook
off the blanket of snow, the snow which covered the
trees and the animals and the straw roof, and your
grandmother stood outside the door of the dancing
cottage, dreaming of America

IF YOU COULD REMOVE THE DEAD FROM THE DEAD

If you could remove the dead from the dead, bomb by bomb, eye by eye, if you could pluck the mad bull screaming, from blood and from dust, from the arena, death unstrung, life returned, the fields of faces, their embraces, like clover, like honey, tooth by tooth like bees in grass, while the generals were not watching i mean, while the dictators were not watching, while the idiotic cheers and jeering of the crowd, while the circular race of steel and money and blood and macho, while the worship of the sword, nobody watching,

Oh it is crazy to think it, oh it is stupid to imagine it, all the sleeping dead rising from death, standing at the bridge, looking down from the parapet, all the incoherent laughter, perfect innocents raised back up from the heap, all the untroubled song, no more disillusionment, no more oblivion, do you understand what i'm trying to say, can you see it for yourself, the slaughtered sons and daughters, sharecroppers and soldiers, students, nurses, peasants and miners, all the sweet lives returned to the living,

And all of us embracing them as they rise, i would have you embrace them, i would have you salute and sing them, and welcome them, the dead from the dead, eye by eye, released from their paralysis, liberated from the uselessness and consignment of their caustic dead sleeping, risen from the junta of dollar and nation and power and design, speaking truth to the ruling class, talking the true talk to those who carelessly plant them into soil,

No not again, no more this root and rock of going! the dead from the dead, taking back their plows and their farmhats, shaking the reins their fathers and grandfathers put in their hands and returning to their work, hands full of seed and dreams and callouses and sweat, can you hear them singing, the song of the living, can you see the morning sun in their beautiful faces, their penetrating smiles, can you feel all that, their small love, their bravery, men and women, risen, children of god again, risen, their mothers' voices softly ringing in their ears,

And am i so stupid as to suggest it, am i so stupid as to imagine it, all their faces in the mist of civilizations and idiotic rain, the dead separated from the dead, bullet by bullet, eye by eye, walking again, hand in hand, like the walking sun

HOW IT WILL END
City by city,
block by block,
in seed and in blood,
this symphony of eyes,
this christening of stars,
village to village,
heart to hand,
you who have taken over
and control too much,
you who have held us down
too long, we will speak out against
you, classroom by classroom, hall
by hall, no death threat can contain
us, no kidnapping silence, this song
we sing, kitchen by kitchen, room by room,
this contagion of the people, this bird which
wants to escape, which must escape, no cage of gold
can hold our discontent, no bullethole of mass distraction,
jail by jail, judge by judge, we will gather up and we will
overthrow you, no government propaganda machine can
shut us down, no fear brigade, no killing crew, no lie of lust
or vanity, and no, not flattery, nothing can stop us from gathering,

Revolution is a small boy reading whitman at a long
wooden table; revolution is a small girl carrying the
book of the world in secret hands; revolution is a young
woman and a young man making love against your terrible
red glare;

And a breeze blows freely through an open door,
and buttercups grow freely through cracked cement,
and we are those flowers and we are that breeze
and we shall not bear your oppression long, the people
we shall wake to our duty soon, the people!
free to stand against you
free to expose you —
snitches and bullies
cowards and thugs —
we shall laugh out loud or die,
we shall beat ten thousand holes
in your useless armor — tank and
troop commander, dictator and hench-
man, informer and border patrol —
and we shall live again, free!

In the precious light of the people's sun
which shines through.

OF TIME HONOR AND MEMORY
Put him out to pasture there is no honor left in him —
old man there is no war literature in your soul only the
memory of guns — can you hear anything beyond that roar

young once something like heroism something like survival

You lived behind an attic door seventeen years, women
fed you — when you emerged you were no longer a man
possessed with the genius of legal murder, possessed
with loyalty to your comrades-in-arms

a bullet flies straight and you carried many men on your back

Those days are gone now and you walk with a cane, like
money walks, and a crooked line goes on for forever and
everyone who knows you gets it — you are already dead —

Emptiness spills from your lungs emptiness is a man
without a family, no longer a man — empty spills into
empty, a rented room is deafening — silence, these are
the guts of an old man's clock

THE ROAD LEADS NORTH ACROSS THE DESERT

The road leads north across the desert until there is no more road only the border wall and that is patrolled by another man in a jeep who throws no shadow. It is the age of helicopter steel. It is the age of the drone and the vigilante, it is the age of fear between men and men, and some men are hollow, hollow as a metal jacket. We do not need more men like that. We need more men like this man waiting for a change in the weather in the desert heat. This man, his hands are shaking with cold, his heart soaking up the world like bread and water. He is a man only a man, but he is making plans to defeat a wall another man has built. And he will defeat it. Kiss the ring and call it holy, where there is work there are men, because there are mouths to fill and the means to fill them. Seal a man in a cactus shell, toss him over the Rio Grande. He will open it up and he will climb back out again.

No one can separate a man from his work, not even a president. A man is stubborn, a man like this man anyway. His breath escapes his body like cold fog, his old life was a prison his new life is a dream, dreams don't die and you can't keep a good man out. He's a leather glove and if you toss him out of a car window and leave him to die his fingerprints will just crawl out and he will keep on coming. He will bounce back, he will cross your fucking border and stand on the corner until someone comes along to give him work and he will nail your roofbeams and spackle your walls, he will put the hinges on your empty coffins.

Cross your heart and hope to die. He is unapologetic, a double fisted immigrant, just like your grandpappy was. His name is immaterial. His name is America.

VISIONS, SIGNS AND BAGATELLES

Visions, signs and bagatelles, a hostile army about to invade a decent town, the walls of an ancient city ruined or renewed, i am always telling myself to listen better, to listen at walls, what happens in walls stays in them, there is truth to the telling, by touch or by sound, in the scent of stone, in the taste of reed, wood and mud on the lips, in the odor of truth, in the tongue placed gently to a wall in darkness, illumination!

How else could the prophets have made prophecy, it is all foretold, and not only walls, the woman at the well, jonah staring into the mouth of the whale, joshua at midnight preparing for war — murder on the flatlands is unthinkable, but may be accomplished without remorse if approved by prophecy,

And words are chains both and the enchained, and words are released by prophecy, from the mouth of a cave, from the mouth of a man, and prophecy is a weapon, a metaphor, a chalice, a stone; and words are drunkards, and powerful, they stagger freely out of the dark of their imprisonment, out into the world — it is madness to presume, madness! to act as if one were a god,

Like a shield that blinds, like a sword that blinds, in the sun or the hideous bursting out of gunfire, to act like heaven and heroes, blind with bloody pride; to carve words into the chest of a dead man's tomb, *here lies mine enemy, whom i slew,* blind;

The throat of a whale is only four inches wide but it swallowed a man whole, and the throat of a man is far narrower than that, and what goes in must also come out, bewildering, beautiful, prophecy; and yet i am always telling myself to listen better, to words in walls, to the sound of them, how cool they feel to the tongue, how full of truth and probity, each word meant to obscure the last, a natural succession of words; words meant to direct, to procure, to supplicate, to subdue;

And the pride of god will strike a man down, i have learned this to my big regret, feeding on grass, crawling nakedly at the pinnacle of noon, my nails sprung like claws, my body sprouting feathers, my back drenched with the dews of heaven;

Therefore go humbly before god and silently, on your hands and knees; therefore learn from your mistakes; therefore know plain truth and no other, speak plain truth, truth spoken plainly;

Truth is sand in shifting sand, barbarians are at the gates of Ninevah

AMERICA THE BEAUTIFUL

Love me like a river she told me and i came unglued and did as i was told like scarlet o'hara in a black and white movie, she was rhett butler which is appropriate to the circumstances she was masculine about the whole thing a ribbon of arrogant light the sun made pretty dimples in her hair

Like it was hollywood popping like it was flashbulbs and coca cola going off all at once atlanta was burning she was the fizz in my champagne and you will forgive me if i admit you this but she had a way of wishing herself into a room and taking it over — a polyamorous majesty which is to say imperious and very male

She was lady romeo all right a takeover queen and i was her next conquest being credulous and in her direct line of sight and anyhow i was focused on my own transgressions so that i did not notice she was shoveling shit like dr. seuss in kindergarden

And i rose up from the bottom like river mud and was immersed i was overcome i was a rainbow trout lying bankside in the great green grasp of the world gasping for air going stiff as a **cocknet.net** novitiate — oh i do love you i said and believed it at that moment — as most men do — and did not care if it was a fraud a phony or an all-american lie

Hook me hard i begged for i will not always be a sucker for your shark charade

CLIMBING MOUNT DIABLO

Blue in her eyes like her husband's blue, pale blue Pacific blue and spreading across the peninsula, in the valley of the Jolly Ho Ho Ho, Green Giant — Green Giant like Dionysus unchained, Green Giant like the host of Moses walking through blue Palestine, Green Giant walking, walking, walking toward the promised land

Like a talmud cowboy kicking up dust and asking no questions, like a uranium prospector lifting up rocks and silent about it, cranky as an entire nation perched on a safety match and hungry for bread and violence, ready to explode, fulminant, fulminant, ready to turn this valley inside out

Yes I have seen that mountain burn, but I have also seen her explode in flowers, a riot of wildflowers in early spring, vivified like Diana at the fountain, quickened like Ruth at the well, many-breasted, able to converse with wild creatures, with the mountain cat, with hawk and with deer, after a cool drink of water I mean, after luminous sex

Fruitful and fierce, dogged out and traipsing along, festooned with shooting stars and manzanita, subtle as rockcress and forget-me-nots, bold as enormous craggy fields of yellow poppies, the full American bop kaballah spreading like crazy heaven across the sky

I have seen storm clouds over suburbia and the Silicon Valley, storm clouds over Del Monte and Hunt Brothers cannery, over the large particle collider, storm clouds over ranchers and vestigial tillages, and over the honest and patriotic Japanese farmworkers lining up for internment

Issei, Nisei, Sansei, whole valleys overspread with hay and fertilizer, the tomato fields of Pleasanton, small children swimming in gravel pits, pumpkin fields and land for sale in Livermore, restless souls near the Rose Hill Cemetery, and beans, beans, pole beans and black, red pintos and cannelini, kidneys and chicks and snaps,

Everything bound for the canneries and the cities of the world,

And yes the mountain, over strangled valleys, sweet as a grace note, lithe as a hummingbird, quick to the kill; and yes, climbing that mountain, flat as a whistle, curling the tongue like butterfly wings, climbing an anchor in the sky, winding and dull, patient for centuries, centuries!

Ready to burst into flame, ready to burst into flower,
Mount Diablo

More magic in its little finger than Jack and his beanstalk —

More music in its heart than the Giant and his bebop horn

CHRYSLER BUILDING IN SNOW
Who ate the neon I don't know but I love New York
always will especially art deco which I take personal for
example the Bronxdale swimming pool where the entire
neighborhood used to swim it's all doctor's offices now
but back in the day

It was a million lanes wide, warm as Miami Beach,
Easter pink and when the swim instructor turned her
back a girl named Ruthie kissed me so hard I got a
nosebleed — it was 1956, whereas this is 2018 a cold day
in January snow falling for two hours and I saw

The Manhattan skyline on the news this morning how
pretty it looks when there's snow in the air, snow ghosts
70 stories up where it's all for show ie the Chrysler
Building on Lexington Avenue which is art deco too
and I read it will be 88 years old in May, world's tallest
building

For 11 months and it took 141 million pounds of sand
silt soil & stone to find rock bottom for the foundation,
my own uncle helped make that hole, they dug 69 feet
down and this year I'll be 69 and okay art deco is dead,
dead as a Sherman Tank crossing the Rhine

And I haven't been to midtown since 2014, eating
oysters with Ruthie, and a lot of the Jews and Italians
have moved out of the East Bronx — but not us — and
the infinite lights of New York City shine for us all on
Bronxville Avenue and Morris Park and Neill

And the Chrysler Building in snow, tall on Lexington
Avenue, sheathed in Krupp's best German stainless steel

WALKING CORDELIA

They were smuggling cocaine on the tall ships it was
1976 it was the birthday of America everyone in high
gear Miami was a living fairytale Miami was a barge
downstream floating among waterlilies and fauna blue
as blue Biscayne — a lifetime of miracles fueled by the
spoon— you were a woman of few words i guess that's
what spells are for — you said if you help me i can help
you — i can part the waters be silent and watch what
happens son, if you can just trust another human being
for one second in your life —

It was the year before snowflakes fell on Southern
Florida that was 1977 and a miracle of its own and
of course i didn't listen i had to spoil the magic — i
never understood much, particularly the drug culture
and anyhow lying on the carpet counting angels was
disorientating — discontent seeps into a room — no need
for words love you said, love doesn't say much — but i
wouldn't listen and I couldn't keep my mouth shut —
hush be silent you said, i was a broken jar of sharp edges
— put your hands to my face — my lips hurt bad —

Breath you said we are made from stars — I saw
crocodiles and exotic fishes i lunged at them wildly —
and the tall ships kept sailing and moonlight parted the
terrible shoreline —

And night shook like all the saints leaving paradise —
you were walking Cordelia —you were a gesture from
the stars that might have passed for love, that might have
cured anything

HOW THE MIST MOVES

To make love to you the way the mist moves, without motive or logic, like a bird of prey, like sufi dancing, like the first man to look beyond the golden valley and feel the urge to go, just go, to stray across the river and go into the glow

I am accustomed to the wind and weather and the city, how heavily raindrops fall on concrete, all the isotopes and jazz, all mad water, and i am accustomed to the eastern sea, its pavilions and concourses, its secret contours and confessions, its corridors of being,

But i have never known the earth like this, in the hands of sun, in my hands, how urgently they rifle through morning — how the mist moves, in search of itself, through your hair, through your clothing, through my impoverishment

And these gestures you offer to the sun and to me, their rhythm, their movement, i have never known gestures quite like these, radioactive, liquid as volcanic rock, quick as obsidian, this sad timepiece ticking in its secret coil and mortal shell

And om to your eyes, and om to your lips, blue nests on mountaintops, and om to this eternal confusion, this thing called infatuation

And i am a man only a man, and you are a category of womanhood i have never known, you reside beyond scandal or desire, unknown even to yourself, and between us daylight grows pregnant and alive, bold as canna lilies and ready to open!

IF ROCKS WERE HUCKLEBERRIES AND EVERY OAK LEAF A MESSAGE FROM GOD

If i had a handful of coffeebeans, and a grinding machine; and squirrels in the yard, and a rifle; and onions and carrots and a sharp knife to cut them up with, and a few potatoes and a little salt, and a clear stream running;

If i had an iron pot and dry matches in a box and tinder in a pan; and shingles and nails and a few sheets of window glass to keep out the rain; and a path to my door and a friend in town with a wagon to visit me once in awhile and relieve the silence, and bring me tea leaves and sugar, and tell me the news;

If i had a tree with hickory nuts and the wind to blow them out of the swaying branches; if rocks were huckleberries and every oak leaf a message from god;

If there was a way to hit apples out of apple trees, safely, i mean, with my fist or with a long stick, so that i could catch them in my hands unbruised, and drop them into a wicker basket well woven by me, and a horse and a hog to share those apples with;

If i had a deep front porch and a straight back chair, and a watchful dog to sit with me and interpret the meaning of storm clouds brewing; and a wife who loved me back, and woke with me up like birds wake me in the morning; and a grandchild learning the alphabet on the floor; you might never hear from me again.

TO COME DEVOTED INTO THE ARMS OF LOVE

To come devoted into the arms of love,
rough hewn, round and weathered,
spooled and unspooled, like thread,
like a dance, played full fiddle
on a golden afternoon; to unwind,
to grow silent and wise, to unfurl
and billow and fill, as in a sail with wind,
as in rafters with hay;

To grow like a well watered garden grows,
to become pitch perfect, like raindrops
on a tin roof, in the manner of rain
dancing on water, swan-throated,
a reflection in a swirl of water,
in the manner of a lake,
imperfection perfecting itself,
what sweet matriculation;

To walk felicitous as love, and rhythmical,
pliant, yielding like soil yields to plow,
like steel yields to the arms of a steelworker,
ankle deep in spark and fire; to stand
at the edge of a horizon, self-composed,
plainspoken as galaxies, to blink back
at the sun, dressed in love;

To lie on a lazy sun-drenched porch,
together, like grain, with you,
together like straw, our hats removed,

full-faced in simple garments,
stitched together like silk;
to be easily buttoned, worn through
but easy to mend — we two,
like stars, lying on our backs,
hand in hand —

We two, eyes to the sun, the big sky mending and
unmending itself above us

IN YOUR HERMITAGE OF WORK OR SLEEP
In your hermitage of work or sleep, where love
cannot touch you, and grief cannot touch you, where
redemption cannot touch you or trouble or hope, where
only the instruments of time, and obligation,

Where i cannot touch you, in your dark hermitage where
you relinquish, renounce, abandon, resign, where you
start all over again, your cell or cloister, your courtyard
of invincibility,

How beautiful! to be left alone! to live religiously and
in sweet seclusion, the news of the world stunning
everyone else, but not you, safe in your deep devotions
and your brethren and mutual exchange of labor,

In your convent of shame and welcome darkness,
undisturbed and why do they even bother to try,
nothing, nothing, you want nothing, only to work and
partake of the bitter pill of duty, forgetfulness and the
distraction of sleep,

in your monks-cap and your cloak of prayer,

There i would touch you, where love lies blind, sleeping
to the touch, where oblivion is a hovering bird and
you ride it like a broom over clay, and you sweep up
everything and the songbird singing

The songbird at your window, at your bedside, the
songbird in the darkness and in your head

the songbird, which would dispel darkness and wake
you to the beauty and the pain of your conscious self, in
the light of the world, singing — the songbird, which has
stopped singing, which wants to sing again

TO HARP DOWN DAY WITH ITS BLOODED NECK
Quite quiet in the late of evening when i am done with
my labor and the mundane offices of day recede and i
am alone as if in a book of prayer, as if a dream may turn
the world inside out, as if in the roundabout confusion
of night which is a book of words i may (finally) get the
words right,

In that moment no death of sleep but an awakening and
i am right with the world again, even where i have been
wrong, remade, the world itself cast in my image, a little
god opening up the book of days and pouring his heart
into it, and in every sentence a world that repairs itself, a
presence affirmed

So that even after blind grappling with earthly forces,
after the mud bark and death of circumstances, even after
paths made and unmade (and what's so wrong with that),
a man is a man and carves his name eagerly into the wild

Because he has to provide or die, even deer do that, and
what so wrong to be a deer among deer, with hands
of torn flesh, mortal and human in the glissando of
sunlight, what so wrong after the cascade of sweat dirt
and stupid mistakes, to sing a sweet dreamsong, to harp
down day with its blooded neck,

After the blood, after the reluctance of stone, i meant to
say, after the skull and bone of mute animosities, and the
branches and thorns that tear your eyes all day, what so
wrong, to lie in silence at last and by dying candlelight, to
give oneself over, devotedly, to love. To god. To eternity.
To you.

LOVE FOLDS DEEP IN THE FOLD

Night of blue mist, night of phosphorescence, night indifferent, chills me to the bone but anyhow pay close attention to the sound night makes, in darkness, under stars, one way or another i have been preparing for this journey my whole life, and maybe you have too, traveling west, discovering each other, drinking a very fine Canadian whiskey, a very nice whiskey from two paper cups

And the western hemisphere rolling past our window like a black and white movie, like two boxers in a ring, circling each other, like a comradeship of hoboes cooking beans over a campfire, this unwritten history which is about to make its play, conflict and defeat and victory, this great escape and somehow i am always miscast, she is too serious or i am too serious, neither of us is movie star material,

But o this is beautiful, you and me,

This time, this disappearance into each other, turn off the meter step out of time, unsure of actual plot or destination but who cares, the massive human tragedy called America rolls and unrolls, engine of its own carnage and self eradication, and the train keeps rolling, train, train, movie screen, this landscape of crickets stars and bounced checks, of iron ore rotting in the belly of the land,

Of orphans and fatcats and losers and winners and
unhappy lovers, and you thread silence and i roll with
the punches, and the progress of love is steady and
private and slow, and on the westbound train love folds
deep into the fold, and time stands still as two deer
across the darkening meadow by a cluster of sycamores,
a small wind shakes the branches, and nothing is sure in
this earth,

The sycamores are watching the deer, we are watching
the deer watch us, and across the table we make love
with tentative hands and the shy kinesis of language
spills like amber around us, and there is a consecration
of good will and sensuous provocation, unleashed from
bedrock, traveling light, traveling light, ignorant of grief,
increasing in confidence and now in full motion — how
long, who knows?

The moment is all and the train is eternal, and love
plunges deep into the world and the world plunges back

And love folds deep in the fold, in unnatural valleys and
silvercast riverbeds, and we are one with you now, world!

And the world shrugs its shoulders and looks away,
heedless of me heedless of you — heedless of love or hope
or destination

TO TAKE YOU UP WHOLE, TO DRINK YOU UP WHOLE
Where trees grow shade, where cattle lowing, where leaf and pebble and cold underground, where water pouring fresh into the bracken, where underground river spilling into a still lake, predator and prey, water spilling!

This is us, somewhere in the middle of the field or mist of birch, this is us in the shyness of deer, a palm tree is hurling curses into the terrible wind, hurricane, hurricane, arc of light, a helicopter is lifting us up, taking us away, the tyrannical army of death is on the march, lift us up into the light,

This is us, I loved you once and heard you everywhere, and you loved me too, and the voice of our bodies was bloodsong singing, and now I cannot see you, cricket wing, and now I cannot say your name, dark palm of a woman,

But I loved you long and love you still, at your work, in your sleep, deep in your cup of womanhood, solitude and regret, though I have reached for you my whole life, like a monk with his lonely chalice of symbols and dreams

to take you up whole
to drink you up whole,
in my mouth, in my blood,
in my body, in the palm
of my hand and the bread
that i break, I take you up
earth, loam bark, rain,
you, lying beside me.

THE CREASE IN HIS SMILE THAT RAN STRAIGHT THROUGH HER HEART

It happened in her younger days, unexpectedly, when the world was magnetic, it was the age of mysteries, and he fell out of the sky and she fell pretty deep for that, an aviator in aviator pants, in for a crash landing, he was standing in front of the house like a question mark in the pole beans, somewhat soft in the prow and anything but majestic, an uncertainty about him but an apparition to her nonetheless, lips like charcoal and pale eyes, too pale, eyes like dwarf valentines, a red-hearted, red-hearted, man, heart sunk deep into his massive chest,

As if he had been stabbed straight through with a bayonet, as if he had been stood out in the rain like an army boot, a rifle butt to the skull, but he had survived and now he was here, a stream of rain pouring from the brim of his hat, into his eyes, down the bridge of his nose, forlorn as a submerged stump, a fossil in clay, and let us be honest his lungs were shot, his liver had already turned into oil, yet a seductive air possessed him for all that, beyond the death and defiance, a familiar air, the crease in his smile that ran straight through her heart, all the way to the state line,

This foolish man and bold, from his belt buckle to his toes, her world was transformed, she could hear her heart beating above the whisper of the hydroelectric dam down at the lake, above the patriotic music on the radio set, it was all jackhammers of desire and static, static, static and okay, and he was crazy as ahab and thick as hemingway, he was a missing shoe in search of its mate, but it felt honest lying next to him, giving him what he asked for, he was only a man but he was the genuine article, southern dawn come to soggy bottom, a man who could match her chronologies and leave no marks,

And she was waiting for a man, without apology or explanation, she was waiting for a man, and without regret, for only one night

HARMONIZING WITH THE CRICKETS
The moon was in leo and jazzlike and slow, a raga of pure existence, and he was just cruising along at a million billion mpg which is to say standing still, doing nothing, a cartoon shiva eating up the zeros, contemplating the stratosphere and true nature of things, because the earth does all the moving doesn't it when you're a hitchhiker among the stars, and you can just stand still, after all what is more rewarding than listening closely to the one song the universe sings, all you got to do is hum along with it, brothers and sisters, sit perfectly still, raging with the crickets and fireflies and axlerods of love, yes! the small sounds of godsong everywhere and nowhere, the cavernous harmonics and universal flood, captivating him, holding him in its thrall,

When he met her, she who was also nowhere and everywhere and of everything at once and a jet trail across the color blue, which is sky, a goddess, a god, a woman, unified as shit, and now it was strong in him, something i mean was strong, and he was tonguetied and alive, a young goat among the columbine, tearing things up, tripping down the clattering shale, and he fell deeply into her, like a river falls into a ravine, like thighs fall quivering into spring, and all attentive to the froth and atmospherics , a cataract from his nostrils to his toes, he leapt like mad-foot nijinksy, sacred in the electro-lab of manmade pizzicato, a slavic ballade of motion in the petri dish of sudden material being, he made love to her headlong and riverine, Man Himself, an action, an intent, an urgency, the biological life force of birth and triumph and tragedy and death, he who after all might alter the trajectory of heaven

THE LYRICAL SPIKE HAS LANDED

Love is a spiral bound notebook carried by an eighth grade girl in pleated skirts wearing pigtails among friends on a roughly swaying school bus, and a knot in the spine of a fifth grade boy on asphalt who has just beaten all the other boys and chased down the rubber ball and now the prize belongs to him and he doesn't know what to do with it;

It is a spoke in the wheel of a bicycle and a space probe in time, and thunder in the dark, and all love wants is a taste of the human condition, a little taste that's all, not necessarily get caught up in it; it is a gimmick, a gadget, a dodge and a device, a lyrical spike in a young man's bottled up brain, the infant upstairs, and a momentary contusion in a young woman's well ordered game;

And you and I are made of cork, and love is a corkscrew, and the corkscrew outlives the cork;

And curiosity is holy, and the heart is a child, a gravitational pull, a garden of love; and love is forever curious, meddlesome and interfering — human really — nosy really, but full of wonder

And love doesn't know the difference between children and women and women and men, and the lyrical spike has landed

DREAM CHILD ILLUMINATES HERSELF

Standing at the corner of 39th and Bell like a river that
flows up she wants to take off her zipcode bandana
and fling it like a flying saucer at the boys in Prospero's
picture window who are gawking at her in their
pheremone hats — none of them can dish like Betty or
beat dawn across the state line — she's too wise for this
shit but she digs the boy who speaks Chinese and went
to Sacramento to sit at the holy knee of Gary Snyder and
she would like to do that too, go to Sacramento, she'd like
to dance like a raincloud full of heaven right out of this
cow town and into The Zen

She is strong and present
nothing can hold her down

too low to the sky, too high for men

PULL AN ANGEL FROM THE FLESH OF MAN

Stop slaying the dragon, man!
listen to the sound of the wind
turning like an egg in a cave,
the hatchling nestled in its
chirping cell, this i mean
is the sound of the rookery
in your head, this is karma,
the sea speaks in parables,
and is plural, the sea is always
naming itself against rocks or
in a perpetual murmuring lagoon
which is monastic and singular
and the mother of god — after all
this experience and death, can't
you accept it? i mean that's your
name in the insinuation of tide

These are the waves which beat
secretly in the veins of every wild
creature and in the treetops, this
the rhythm, surreptitious flowing,
your blood your bones your court-
yard of silence, your greatest poem,
this is silence — unpronounceable!
stealthy as a fossil, persistent as a
snail crawling in the muddy shoals —
strong as parchment paper i mean
entire armies march helplessly against
armies, they fold, all of them — it avails
them not — soldiers and generals,
ignorant philosophies!

And an ocean breaks and dies,
an ocean returns to ocean heaven,
and you are ocean and are reborn,
coexistent in the salt soup and
shade of every cell and membrane
under the sun

Excellent! every microbe swimming in the sea of existence

And when your eyes gone blind
and when your skin transparent
and in the dark when you think you
are lost in the labyrinth of dreams
this is your poem, too — a mortal
entanglement germinated
in the cave of all being

Surf against surf, sand against sand —
blade, leaf, iron, inkblot, grass — rabbit
hole and mask of clay — whetting stone
and water bead — hand against hand
heel against heel, I tell you stop slaying
the dragon man!

Pull a lion from a rock, a leviathan
from a shell — pull an ocean from
a wave a cloud from the belly of a
serpent, pull a dandelion from a
dandelion seed — pull an angel
from the flesh of man

Pull a dragon from the heart of me

YO SOY MECAPALLI

I am a working man, servant of the field, call me *campesino, soy mecapalli*, the *macehualli* in my chest makes furrows of clay, husband of this land and a wife besides, the mission and the ranch also sleep beside me, and beans for trade or on my dinner plate, plain as a spoon, plain as a dish of wooden crosses and Guadalupe comes to me and plants corn in my ear, her eyes are silver and benevolent, I do not look upon her, our saints told us that, our teachers told us that

Our parents told us and our priests and our books, do not look upon her so I do not look and I am humble before the mother of god, I spit into the palms of my two hands and take up the plough, and the soil in the crease of my hand is rich, and my heart grows like garden roses, my heart where the cold of stars pulses hot and in the front room where my sons are young, my heart is there and in the valley which rings with their laughter, they come and they go, their legs are strong, *nuestro muchacho* — do they serve themselves yes, and I am proud of them, their indifference, their usefulness, society offers them nothing and they respond in kind, the government offers them nothing

And I can hear them singing, and the wild animals can hear them, and the corn hears them singing and that is my heart, my sons shouting and singing and the ranch sheep that look up, and the sun hammering in their faces, sun beaten bright as copper — and my daughters too, fragrant as incense, flowers, their sweetness and

their complexity — and the zapote tree which is shadow
to lizard and dust, and the seed of the sapodilla which
hooks in my throat if I am careless, and when i am deep
in the horizon and raw and alone I can hear the boss of
other men in other fields, *jefe!* speaking to other men,
he wears his white hat and i wear mine and the river that
flows between us wears white rays of sunlight

And i carry you on my back like firewood, Guadalupe,
I gather you in my arms and cross that river, and
sometimes I pull mesquite from my mouth and
sometimes cactus flowers, and sometimes I pull death
out of my mouth and sometimes resurrection — from
my mouth, like children, from my mouth, like teeth,
like copper coins or language or payment in kind,
and I gird myself and go back to work, girdle of rope,
leather strap that binds us, I bind myself in devotion to
you, Guadalupe, to you, compassionate, patient, round
mother of god and pure as tears

I an onion, I born in a cemetery and destined for the
cook pot, I a simple man to be cut up, boiled and eaten,
but my throat is heaven, and when I do look up I see
your face Guadalupe and I am rain to a rockpile, and a
quarry hollowed of stone, this is my song and it rings
with the voices of working men, and this is my offering
to you, church of morning glory, *yo soy mecapalli,* shovel
in hand, yet if you cut me I will cut back, hard, and my
tongue will be a talon when it is not drawn in, my blood
bright as stars and hot as piss in a pail, piss and milk and

rust, and a little hole in the land is where snake lives and that's better than nothing, especially to snake, especially to *los magueyitos*

And if I sleep I dream and if I dream I am a man, a man may eat bread

Mi casa, mi hija, mi madre — my offering table, tlamanalpechtli ofrendras, I lay flowers at your feet when it is morning, I swallow my sleep and return to the river and the river flows east

And in the rush of morning and in the wings of birds I am wings too, I am river bank, wedded to river and land both, and in the upland grass I am buckles and wire, tan as tea —

ve y cultivar la tierra

Your voice is a bell and the blood in my temple sings, *tlatzitzilitztepuztli*

ONE GREEN ACRE OF SUMMER CORN

This is improved land, tall, made even, lost in itself,
spread out, steady to the touch, fresh as pie, responsive
to the rolling pin, as in a young girl's smile, as in the
sweet-burr of tousled hair running with the schoolboys,
as in new daisies on the verge, under the right man's
hand land like this may yield its fortune, regenerate,
hard soil returns to the plow and I do not fear god or
man, and I do not fear the government, and if I keep
one eye open to the weather that's because a handsome
propagation rewards the constant hand

And this earth is good to us still, and I love you like
a field of pumpkins that needs steady picking —
strawberries rhubarb watermelon eggplant, seedgrapes,
it is all the same, the whole earth shines purple in the
yellow sun and shucks itself clean of death, and if I could
roll you up by hoof or by hand I would do it, i would do
it and patiently, I would handle you in rows, one row at
a time, steadily, and that would be fine, the good earth
understands a man like me, it is a mystery and I do not
wish to question it or lay waste to it

And yes these are my father's hands, stronger than a
wolf trap and coiled like ship's rope, and yes these are
my mother's hands, stronger than a claw hammer (her
long stride equine in the galloping field, her long gaze
a furrow of busted up knob-root — gravel, pumice,
riverloam, silt, topsoil and clay, goddess among the
crowfoot, her womb a harder soil than what most men

around here could vision or count on or manage, her
body a kind of a well that yields itself up if treated right,
her body well watered, top dressed, dug back under —
my mother, her body, her hands)

And yes the magpies are at the dogdish sometimes, and
yes the bees drone like hobos among the appletrees; and
yes plow parts rust in winter and all that western snow;
but this land returns to its senses in spring, and there's
seed corn in the jar, though the barn mice take their
share — and yes we could call this valley Resurrection if
we wanted to and we could find our way together, you
and me, if we wanted to; right here in this valley where
there is no taking without giving back, right here in this
valley, where there is this laying out properly, and these
sweet straight rows

This ministration and this yield — one green acre of
summer corn

BLACK ANT ON A COUNTERTOP, TWO DEER IN A YELLOW FIELD

Black ant on a countertop, two deer in a yellow field, no not the yellow of mown hay, it is too early in the year for that, barely June and it's early morning and sunlight yellow as new baked bread, and she is upstairs and I want to tell her everything but if I make a noise they will bolt, even through window glass they can feel me, and I can feel them, in my fingers and in the pit of my stomach, and something is rising in my limbs and coursing into my shoulders and hair, I cannot say a word or move, I'm holding my breath even as milk swirls white in my coffeecup

And I saw these two in November when the meadow grass was taller than a man and ready to die, and there was six months less gray in my hair and six months more time on my clock, and the yellow field was fragrant with seed and sunlight petrified the world in its unholy amber gaze,

But now it's spring, sunlight dips a finger into itself and is precarious, sunlight slips over the meadow and paints two deer, mated by caution, keen in appetite, regal in manner, and each ear a spoonful of dolloping sun; and the meadow spreading out its welcome mat, thick as yellow butter, thick beyond yolk, yellow beyond butterfly wings, utterly unlike the green of the woods beyond, which is deep and inviting,

And every forest was virgin once and will be again, and every spring can renew the compact between deer and ants and men, and I do not wish to disturb the deal and I want to be true to the nature of things, all the gods and goddesses are involved, and I wish to have these two deer run freely through my existence, like all the wild women who have danced freely through my existence and kept on going, leaving me astonished, empty, exhausted and renewed, leaving me blue,

Yes, these two deer groomed by mystery and circumstance, yellow dappled and sunlit, raised in secret places and therefore holy, and I wish I could find the crayon that is their exact color — burnt siena, umber, chestnut, ambergris — and put it to the tip of my tongue and swallow it; and swallow every color in the world — the color of a black ant on a countertop, the color of two deer in a yellow meadow; the color of her — as if she is not lost to me, as if the sound of her slippered feet upstairs awakens innocence, as if I can endure her smile.

LONE STAR LOLLIPOP

loyal as a lollipop crazy as a mule, call me the original texan, more powerful than a lone little star, fuck you and your stupid flag! these are the voyages of the starship anahuac, faster than an armadillo more powerful than an oil well, I drew me a blackbean I won me a farm, I drew me a bead on mister mexicano and now look at us here we are, the lone star state

blam baby blam

this land is my land and there's a prize in every box and texas is the biggest one of all a major league pop up, boy this land it'll melt in your mouth and I have heard tell

how your granpappy got to shoot em up big a few years back that was 1843 and he did it with his paw's little peashooter

that's some neat little davey crockett stunt that's trix in a box and gives you the right (ie second amendment)

step right up keep a steady hand! stand in line mister put your head into the patriotic restoration slot machine — this is texas if i want i can stick a shotgun up your ass and call it legal i can wall you out and wall me in, I can call this a nation — hang you your mother your brothers and all your sister's kids, you can all go back to the rio grande

i don't pay it no mind and i don't pay no attention — nor
to the little man behind the curtain with the little hands
and orange hair

just do what the border officers tell you and nobody in
this truck will get hurt (lord sake salute the flag. And do
not take no knee honey)

sixteen rangers all in a row — sixteen rangers & everyone
a horse marine 16 soldiers & one of them rowed out into
copano bay & blew hell out a cargo ship full of mexican
damn guns & that gives you & me the right

sixteen soldiers and it was one of them's birthday & sorry
i was, not to be one of them to help him celebrate with
whiskey and cake

and i don't know your lingo but i know your hooch like
i know your women and yes ma'am i was taught better
than that you do not take what does not belong to you

but there's bills to pay and little mouths to feed and land
to be had and when the sky goes hot i pray for wind it
is only natural and when the creek goes dry I pray for
butterflies because the grace of god is mine

just pray the white man don't go postal again, not on you
this time

and gregorio cortez was farming nr kenedy texas in 1901 when the sheriff and his boys, mounted men, rode up and questioned him about a stolen horse and cortez didn't have no stolen horse and his brother stepped out of the tall grass so they shot him dead

and if god is justice i will leap out of the tall grass someday and i will plow them down, sheriff and men

I will fill their old graves with new blood

GYORGY KASTRIOTIS

A river can unite or divide us; a river may follow the land, or carve the face of the land into pieces, separate the people from each other. And Skanderbeg was a river, and the land too — Gyorgy Kastriotis! A large man on a large horse. Skanderbeg, who could not be defeated!

With his horse and his sword, with his heart and his name; the stroke of his sword could bring forth spring waters; the hoof of his horse could carve his name in solid rock. Gyorgy Kastriotis, who married Donika Arianiti, forging a single nation out of the separate tribes of men.

(and the Lake of Flowers, into which the women of Albania threw themselves rather than surrender to the enemy, blows chilly and cold in the Lura Highlands). Skanderbeg! Whose golden helmet floats more golden than gold over Albania!

And a river runs thru Albania, the Shkumbin River, and the enemy built a fortress there, and Skanderbeg tore it down. The enemy put siege to Shumbat and Oranik, and Skanderbeg defeated them. The enemy slipped through the Drin Valley, and Skanderbeg built a bulwark against them.

Skanderbeg could not be defeated! But Skanderbeg died, and the enemy took hold of the land. And some of the people spread like seed on the winds of the world, and some of the people remained. And Albanian poppies grew thick and red and black in the fields, and the conquerors remained until they were gone.

And now, on the flag of Albania, red and black, there is an eagle. An eagle, double-headed and proud.

And I am a shepherd boy, I play a shepherd song. I am man with a clarinet, I play kaba for the wedding parties. I am qiftali, a two-stringed instrument, boys and men play me equally on the banks of the Shkumbin River and laugh in the dancing wind.

My first string is the heart of the people. My second string is the voice of Skanderbeg.

And wherever the Albanian people gather — in fields and villages, in Balkan cities, across the great diaspora of the world — wherever the Albanian people gather in their going, they say this, concerning Gyorgy Kastriotis:

> *Skanderbeg! who could not be defeated! you give me honor, you give me the name, Albanian.*

And the wind blows freely over the plains of Shumbat.
And the wind blows freely over the plains of Oranik.
And the wind blows freely thru this song, red and black
The wind, singing like a river that can unite or divide us.

EIGHTH DAY RISING

Eighth day rising, day of the poet and the dreamer,
day of birth and rebirth and wisdom and healing,
day of the gallows and the baptismal font,
of myth-maker and mosaic, Orpheus at his lyre,
Arachne the mortal weaver at her loom

Day of goat-herd and thresher, day of grape grower
and his sacred vine, given by the gods and taken
by them too, day of the wild creatures drawn from
wild places to what is surely holy, the fantastical
made flesh, where myth meets moment

And — drawn more strongly than most — creatures
of forest and field, creatures of wild places and the
chimeric, come to places set apart not by man or
by church, nor consecrated by custom or kind
but by the pure animal abracadabra of devotion itself,

Untainted and unscripted as nature, the original
and instinctive — deer and dove, poet and elk,
the drummer at his drum, the bird at his wing,
immaculate, visionary, frenzied, becalmed —
the dancer who triumphs over dizzy pain,

The Thracian at his solitary potters wheel

All creatures who yearn for free-flowing waters,
all creatures who seek the source and well-spring
of earth's first song, which offers up, in its sweet
implacable flowing, the scent and substance of eternity

Freedom from the bonds of death.

NOT THE VARDAR

Are you ready for this, no not the Vardar, never the Vardar, shit in the fountain, anarchy on a silver plate, here comes blood in the baptismal font, here comes addiction in the wishing well, this city is a streetdog sleeping under a mulberry tree, who said Troy, who said Skopje, or Athens or Rome, any city really, one that does not shine, one whose colors fade, whose streetlights do not glow, no matter what alphabet,

St Cyril did not mean for this, nor priest nor professor nor founding father, innocent rage, justice at the end of a bayonet, coming in low to heaven and coming in fast, revolutionary message in a plastic cup, more than any oligarch can stand, call me armored vehicle, call me tear gas and riot gear, call me the graffiti in the parking lot, this is my spray paint, my name is alias and I am drone-dark but not so dark as night, nor so endless or without hope as fascism,

But yes, black in the mouth, and the sirens in the lungs and the confusion in the heart are hot, and get one thing straight I'm for real and in your head, I am a working man curses, I am a student who kisses the mouth of death and only half hates it, the flower merchant is my ally, and the painter in his studo and pickpocket, boneweary and polluted, cheap perfume to cover it all up,

You call this home, you call this the devil himself, who would smoke this dope, this river of ashes that swallows up farm and forest, swallows up factory and trail and apartment block and gallery, spits it all up, not the Vardar of course, not Vardar, any river Stalin's river, Khrushchev's river, Trump's river, this river of empties that floats by like toy sailboats, like slaughtered Argonauts, gangster bodies in a gangster river, no colorful tricks or movie pranks, no heroism,

A sediment of blood at the bottom, pit and wing and eyes of a magpie, beaten men, beaten women, and boiling like sausages, and foraging, foraging, on its rapid way to the sea.

THE HEART IS A GOOD SOLDIER IT KEEPS ON TICKING

Lazarus was more than a man, you know,
and a heart is a good soldier it keeps on ticking —
more than just a part of the body, certainly —
amore, amore, you cannot stop a beating heart
in English or Italian and what does it even mean,
a heart? It means when a heart skips a beat
love fills it in, and this the measure of a man,
how love fills him in, this is his cadence, because
a man who pays attention to his heart draws water
from a well

When Lazarus lay dead in a cave Jesus pressed his fingers
to the dead man's lips and his heart burst back to life

And a man who is touched by love knows no limits
and bursts back to life no matter what, and what is
the body compared to this —

That in a nutshell is where I'm at these days

And when someone is standing on his head
looking through your window, when someone is
just standing there without moving, like a deer
in a burning forest trying to figure his way into
or out of this human mess, that's a sign, that's a sign,
it tells you there's something is about to happen
and you've gotta pay attention to that

Joy beyond pain, hope beyond death, like no animal
existence or instinct man has ever known —

O numberless beating beats of the human heart —
o heart itself — a man who dies twice does not die
at all, he is Lazarus, he comes back to life, reborn

ASS FORWARD THRU OCEANS

Who in the alley? blood. Who in the church aisle? blood. Who in the workboot the hymnal the corral? Who in the vestry who in the grave, who in the bunkhouse in the last lost Las Vegas gambling den?

And standing naked and proud on the human trafficking auction block, who?

Workers women children and men.

Blood racing through centuries, blood for the slaughter blood for the sacrifice blood for the restless rich man and his cotton and impeccable missus blood for the work crew boss what he does he fears what can we do to kill him, take what he possesses, the will to dominate to own to increase his estate, to tear to shreds a great continent unchallenged by greed until he is choking in it, the hooves an endless trail of dust and blood a silent swale of avarice like branding irons.

Your skin my skin what's the difference all of us born one under god and the animals too and the spinning wheel.

Cover it all up.

II
And I called her desert flower and she called me Pecos but she was no flower no dream she was actual cactus and my name was Pete, she was a mule skinner's daughter thick chested like a barrel of nails fallen off

the back of a California pickup buried in the 20th century but resurrected more recently and put up on an American pedestal.

The least dead chick of the bleached bone bleacher seat patriotic set.

III
O what is this the wages of manifest destiny yes you gringo caught in your own stirrups dragged 3000 miles from coast to coast bloody and blind and the Red River rolling thru Texas and the Rio Grande thru chaparral, O what is this? Gazed down upon lovingly by Janus, the two-fisted god of jewels and chains and a moneybelt besides, harder than clay, a two armed murderess eyes like head lights on a desert that has seen no rain in centuries.

IV
Desert and desert and desert flower. I called her that at first.

And at first I could not move, my limbs were stiff from the sun and her gaze too strong at first she was a fixture like stone, a statue or mist of Mesquite, a petroglyph, but then my tiny heart like a mosquito began to stir, which was worse.

And that caused the rain clouds to form.

And we got rain.

V
Passed through window on the way to raindrop. Passed through raindrop on the way to sky. Passed through thunder on the way to stars. Stars to clouds a pretty passage more beautiful than standing still and decidedly non-linear, a movement akin to liberation, the illusion of passing through

Does a cloud even know it is a cloud, of course not. it is not anthropomorphic it's a cloud.

Mystic cloud, ghost cloud, cloud born in a river of Aztec gods, cloud more powerful than redwood, than all the iron ore in the bowels of earth. Border cloud of bursting rain and god the punisher of all Earth's captors.

VI
Passed through lightning passed thru time passed through the miserable sky on the way to freedom, an illusory ocean of our own selves.

Our Many selves, limitless.

Which is no contradiction or metaphor but the ur-intelligence of culture or race, spoken in the proto language of our ancestors, all we should ever need or require and an actual human fact.

To know to feel to love.

VII
We've come a long way to end up here, where we started from. Where am I headed? Ass backward through oceans on the way to myself.

And I am cloud like you, electric! And I am the light and the darkness which is the blood of your cloud. It is my being! and I like it that way.

THE FELLAHEEN WHO SAUNTER THROUGH OPEN MARKETS

The fellaheen who saunter through open markets in exotic places trading spices and pearls, bargaining for perfect pears, the beautiful men, beautiful women, peasants and indigenes and I was always a stranger in a strange land, in the drug store in the camphouse in the bodega the cafeteria the dormitory the barracks but never never stranger than this, living below sea level the poverty line and outside the law but at least the radar of America cannot touch us here

A SHADOW WHICH HAS BEEN FOLLOWING US A VERY LONG TIME

And this is how it works, earth speaks every tongue, we speak none of them, or at least only a few, having been raised up in some particular place, having been taught by others to talk like them, having absorbed a few sounds as we made our way to or from school or church or jailhouse, from grandfathers and cousins and creekbeds, from the pirouette of ice in an abandoned lot and from treestump and blue mountain range, from stovepipe and that strange apparition in the park, and the rusty links of cold chain swings, cold to the touch,

This is how it makes itself known, new lands passing thru old, old lands passing through themselves, all of them intersecting in every atom and cell and yes in our being and if we are open to it and if the elements collide, then we can hear perhaps earth, speaking in every tongue, pick up a word or two, or maybe a phrase, if we can just turn a corner at the right time i mean, and walk facefirst into the impossible song of an unexpected ocean, a whirlwind or a hurricane or a drought

Or looking up at the mad utterance of the wind hear earth's voice, finally. as it passes through unfamiliar trees, fire! or at sunlight as it comes down to us through clouds formed somewhere very far from us while we were going about our business unaware, and hearing for the first time, we open our mouths to speak, our first authentic syllable! burst from clouds and atmospheric pressure building, a shadow which has been following us a very long time is in the moment of its true birth and coming,

And this our wonder, and this our great inheritance, inspired
through skin and nostril, through the buttocks, through fine
follicles of invisible body hair, caught and consumed and
bristled and fully inspired and taken in, simply, until the
very footsoles of our being are reciting indelible phrases and
passages. and soot and soul and the sweet language of walking
immense distances, and the language of remaining behind,
unshod with the horses, and the language of moving, and
standing still

And what manner of man is it who'd go through this world
alone and speechless, through creek bed or dead arroyo, what
manner of man with no words for prayer, what manner of
man, disappearing into a cathedral of pine, perishing of thirst
in guineafowl territory while searching for a lost mining
camp, or eldorado, perishing for want of words or snatched
voiceless from a nest and sent sailing seed by seed with the
dandelions.

To learn this new earth-language, take root snakelike and
shaking us by the short hairs and making us its own!

O silent expressionless face o blossoming animus o sudden
majestic new-song!

Language known and absorbed,
language natural and alien the
same, earth language, reaching
through our spines and stomachs
and out of our brains, urging our
stupid wagging tongues to speech.

GRAZING LIKE CATTLE BETWEEN SPECKLED GRASS AND SKY

There was a name for this thing once, when it began,
a word like patience, a word like silence, but not the
sleeping kind, not empty-hearted unkind or alone, a
name like rattlesnake, cactus, trance, divine, a word from
which all language comes, like love — in the beginning
I mean, not only human language but language of
animals, language of gestures and shapes, language like
shadow of wing, like fist or claw, a language we used for
god before there was a god, a word we will use for god
after god is over, a syllable or a sound, a name like echo
which is another name for wind.

And there was another name for this, when it began,
a word like selfish, a word like appetite, a word like
fear and the slick spread thick on the tongues of the
lugubrious, a dull word harsh to the ear, harsh as
helmets, hard and cruel, knowing, crafty but dull as a
boot, the wrong end of the stick, a busted broad axe and
at the heart of this thing, where it was written in blood,
where it was cut from the mouth of a woman and baked
into tablet clay, it rang in our ears until there was a
plainness everywhere, plain as a poison apple, a poison
you can't resist that can cure nothing and cannot be
cured by prayer.

And now this solemn, this sanctimonious, and now this
heartless grace — this duality!

And mankind sticking to the skin when touched, and
mankind burning the palms of the hand, and the word
for justice no better than strappado and rack and the
word for mercy no better than a spike thrust into the
side of a crucified man.

que gacho, the wound is still bleeding.
que gacho, another nation is in exile —

grazing like cattle between speckled grass and sky.

ONE EARTH ONE PEOPLE

The more I sleep
The more I dream
The more I dream
The better I pray
So listen to this —
Here is the wall
Here is the people
No one can say it
better than that —
Here is the smoke
rising like a church
rising like campfire
rising like a kitchen fire
rising like the border
that separates us from
each other and blinds us,
town from town, pueblo
from pueblo and ranch
and farm animal and
farm family — each from
each — the smoke that blinds
us, the people who crossed
borders to just be with
each other, to just live with
each other decently. No!
Nobody knows this better
than us. This is no border.
This is the front line in the
war against lines and no one

can tell us what walls we
should build between us.
Walls! Inside us, around
us, behind and in front of
us. So many walls! Ridiculous!
I'm surprised we haven't all gone
blind and no one knows this better
than us, here where the people
are undivided, where the people
rise up like rivers and join together
with heaven to form one great
river, united as the sea — to eat
to laugh to work and to prosper,
and to pray together, because the
more we pray the better we dream
— one earth one people —
a wall which is no wall is a river
that is no river at all — and we are
that river, one people, here and
everywhere we go, reverential,
strong, better than what anybody
takes us for, and what do they know
about us, we flow along and we listen
and we dream — and nobody can stop
us from doing that, nothing and nobody.
No borders! No walls!

Open your hearts
  Open your doors
Out come the people

CENDRAR'S MONKEY

To see animal-heaven in every direction, to see owl-like and ask no questions, to have no human direction and finally understand, to be the animal replica of my own design, a thing unseen on any cave wall painted by any man, to sing the song no caged animal has ever sung, no Easterlamb skewered on a roastng spit, no animal rotated in its own sweet sweat and pungent juices, nor Blake's crazy Tyger nor Schubert's idiot trout, no swimming upstream against a wind quintet,

No huffypuffy wolf no cartoon pig with blunderbuss, no Lascaux beast or Whitman and his stage-prop butterfly

To sing the song of the loping horse, the jackrabbit of Nevada, the song of the creature never resurrected, not Phoenix-like not Christ-like, never called upon to rule over ruined Nations, nor albatross nor tim'rous wee beastie, nor felonious among the lotus blossoms or secret in the wet blue mildew hayrick beside the willow tree, no mascot for fratboy pranks, no Cendrar's drugged monkey and no Cat in a Hat hookah-smoking caterpillar, not even an alphabetical animal in Apollinaire's otherwise excellent bestiary,

And no more subject to the serious business of man — to build to imagine to rule to interfere — because a man may be reincarnated a creature superior to a man!

No hooded bird of prey on a knight's tournament
sleeve, no errand boy hound or armor crest, no shield
of protection no guardian of unknown uncouth cities
littered along the Mediterranean — to fly to swim to run
— to burrow in Arctic earth, through skull and spine and
shoulderblade, through Norse helmet and beneath the
snowblind trail of migratory tribes and Asiatic nomads,

Creature that slides through everglades
Creature that is unleashed by Artemis
Creature of terrible retribution, ravenous
Om! the silence of death in weeping air
Om! my blood my flesh my appetite
Om! my wild mane and unbraided hair
and my brains of Pegasus and my deadly
tusk of the rampaging Caledonian boar

Sheep that Cyclops never tasted, Ruse that Odysseus never
employed, free in the naked darkness to my own being,

An animal that does not fit into the ovens of men or around
the necks of women, an animal that blinks and whole armies
of soldiers disappear from fields of battle or are drowned,
Pharoah's armies, Jericho's armies, dying louder than the
bleat of any ramhorn blown by man,

I want to be the eagle that escapes every day from its cage
and tears freely at the air, the eagle that sits at the right hand
of god and watches in the tall branches, the leopard in its
spots the salmon on its blind run home,

Beyond the lure of bait or self sacrifice, the urban antelope the attic invader the feral cat just waiting for a man around here to make some mistake, beyond the reach of slingshots and firemen and game wardens, of cops and criminal mischief makers, beyond the reach of shoot em ups and handlers and Hollywood grips, of the cries and caresses of the zookeeper's curly-haired daughter

I want to be an animal with long tooth and yellow claw that bites back when it is bitten upon, that scratches its neck and a host of fleas stand up and applaud, halo'ed with flecks of golden sunlight, an animal whose natural tattoo is original grace, whose kindness reveals itself in the nubile movement of haunches, whose destiny is nests and aeries, and in the tunnels and gray shining pools of water that elephants drink from speaks in a voice as hushed as bushberries, and the savannah wind rustling and playing, and a gray good parting at dusk,

I nuzzle through the low branches
I graze through the evergreens
I am on my way to human-free
essence of pure animal existence,
unmoved by snare or by muzzle,
unmoved by beating drum, unmoved
by lure or by spear or cage or blind

Unmoved by the lonely calls and music of mortal men.

WATCH ME BURN IT TO THE GROUND IN THE TALLGRASS, BABY

This is how to bounce in the free world baby
tall in the tall grass this is how to live on the
edge this is how to put down the gun pick
up the groove and fear nothing, live on the
outside — this is how to walk the liberation
walk make a big ugly footprint in the lily
white snow —

This way next stop new existence, exit stage
right from the systematic FBI ass-fuck tent

Exit this way to the skyblue limit to the road
for eagles — exit this way, get out of the way,
meet me in the next century it looks like it's
going to get ugly around here because it is,
let's just keep passing thru, don't try to stop
us motherfuckers.

I do not care what your church of trump got to
say i do not care what your evangelical squeaky
clean russian hooker church of golden shower
hypocrisy got to say —

Take your redneck handshake take your wall
street three piece take your rich boy bodysuit
and frack it.

Take your filthy money and stick it back in your
pocket, what's money got to do with it — you
want to walk that way then go ahead but keep
your hands off a free man's groove —

And guess what if you build a wall it'll swallow
you up whole and leave you rotten and the rest
of the planet free, and if you want to know
the truth i know my enemy and it's you.

I ain't going to say nothing you say i ain't going to oblige.

Because no i am no problem child but i do not
subscribe no not to your fascism not to your greed
no not to your how-to who-to when-to what-to —

What did it ever get anyone in the end except headlines —

And who's gonna stop me? no not you mister
groovecop no not you mister talk show fox news
tv propaganda queen.

No not you mister swear on a stack of bibles
robot, mister right wing dope blind hashtag
chalkmark tweet-a-minute prison yard bigot.

Guard me all day long if you want to reverend
nobody — no one gonna tell me what.

Watch me burn it to the ground in the tallgrass. baby.

LAVENDAR TEE AND DOGTAG CHAIN

Resurrection is a gift to the young, and of the young, there is a man inside a man, a young man of thirty-two or thirty-three wearing a lavendar tee and a dog tag chain, and i am that man, and i am not done with this thing yet, roll away the rock! you cannot kill the man inside the man, what you think will kill a man only makes him stronger;

And i am a thug a feline a warrior a lover, i land on all fours and am with you and born again, surge of sex, quick swing of an ax that cleaves wood, a male in full song and this scar on my neck is a proud wound, and this constant flow of fresh blood engulfs me, i am pierced and that sweet hiss which follows dissipation is my mating song;

Inside or outside a man's body it is all the same, sweat or sway a man is an idea of a man, death is reprieve and renewal, spring will return and the season flow, and there is a woman who walks inside a man, any man who knows anything worth knowing knows this, even as he walks to his own rhythm, roll away the rock get ready for the resurrection;

And rising through the marsh and meadow in search of a mate is a spring bird, and i am that bird, talkative, living, alive, and i have landed in the meadow and have a tale to tell, and i am waiting in the marsh, i am the redwinged blackbird's sweet toowhee and sung in many a fourth month, the last snow falling is a songbird in the budding bush;

i have been moved by and i move the world, roll the rock away!

I fly away and i return. the mist of the worldsoul is my spring and my mist, and spring returns, and i return.

Life's no ending, winter holds no dominion, resurrection is a gift to the young and of them, christ keep singing to me.

YOU AND ME DAD
Looks like this year might be different, you and me dad on a
two man holiday, it's a guy thing just the two of us cruising
like we used to do when you were alive, before grandma got
the flu and grandpa ran off with the chambermaid — oh i
got no room for moral judgement, skepticism works fine for
me now, i have studied the naked men and the wise, and the
gymnosophists are singing to me let's go dad, let's go dad,

I can hear their voices in the mirror, there's a shipwreck
on the mountain, a shipwreck on top of a shipwreck in the
hudson river and i know what happens to ordinary men at
the bottom of the world harbor

This planet is a fire breathing bull and who's got the answer,
absolutely not you and me but so what man, comets are
more spectacular than the sun, what is a man to do except
dig for dionysus, take the quick ride with the scythian
horde, go highwire and wild on wine weed and honey,
transgress the caucasus and who needs a horse when a man
has wings, wings! the world is rich, so rich, even in the
midst of mud and quarries,

Snapping turtles and kingdoms of gold, unnamed
continents, blue skies over the aleuts and me and you,
six miles higher than an etruscan helicopter and half the
distance to the goal line,

Yeah it looks like you and me this year, this year might be
different for you and me dad, spanning the hellespont, you

and me gonna spar with judah, go two rounds for ten, had
enough of this dad well so have i, spun like a river of big blue
cadillacs, let's go dad i'm gonna pay for it all in cash and put
down the top, strap you in and set this hunk of junk on fire
and who needs a map when i got you and you got stars in
your eyes

No harm no foul, i got my geiger counter working overtime, a
working man's life's all right i suppose even a chemical dump
has its purposes but lately there's been rats in the pantry, too
many asses in the grave, you've been dead since '93 and my
gas tank's on empty (yeah it could be the gauge) so let's go
dad!, me and you, circumnavigate the palatine that's the plan,
you and me in our cosmogenic rocketship — lisbon paris
kandahar tenerife — atlantic city

Baby i don't care baby you and me — fist full of honey and
let's go spelunking the rockies, dig up the karmic candlestick,
goathappy and stupid as a couple of roman soldiers throwing
dice at the feet of the nazarene

We have done our time nose deep in the bottomless ocean
we have done our time diving shipwrecks in the lonely old
hudson, where's my golden cross for it all?

Still it might be something different for us this time, you & me
dad, if we play our cards right, if we don't do what we are told
one time — you and me dad, two damn peas in a single pod,
you and me, dear old dead old dear old dad —

This earth don't hold a candle
to you and me

GOOD MORNING RAINBIRD WITH OCEAN IN YOUR WINGS

It could be any ocean, any ocean, but it is this ocean, the pacific a supple beast of air, and you could be any bird, but you are rainbird with ocean in your wings, whalesperm in your bones, turtleshell in your buttpack and a walrus tusk in your pistol belt, born of a volcano and the hillsides of Southern California burn for you, the canyons of central coast are pregnant with the coldblood and winesap of your mother, and you are rainbird but volcanobird too, the cliffslides of Big Sur worship you, Monterey falls face forward into the mud before you, you are a rosetta stone of sanskrit and mandarin, entire histories of humankind travel in your belly, entire generations of extinct creatures fester in your bowels, species of the crawling depths,

Rise up from the seabottom, rainbird! you seize your prey like the jade creature of myth, bright mother of pearl kestrel with your animal elegance, strange as a sea cucumber, voracious bird, ruthless as European civilization, rusty as the hull of an iron warship, abalone bird with a breast like a one quart canteen, i have seen the bullet in your eye, i have felt your peeling wind ready to strike, porous and post apocalyptic, bird of rain, forager of the dunes, voracious and voracious and foul, you could eat anything rainbird but you eat fishegg and squid, you eat crustacean, you eat ligament and bone and plastic plucked from Oregon garbage cans,

And it could be any bones but it is these bones, Jack London's bones and the bones of coyote eating crickets and i have seen Cortez rising out of the marrow of your bones, like old Oakland,

raucous, macho, classically colonial, like squid rising to the
surface of an ocean at night, elegant! and i have seen oil
merchants in their lonely pursuit, whale oil, crude oil, and
Teddy Roosevelt on the malarial shore, it is all the same — and
i have seen the bifurcated starlight guiding your way east, it
could be any star but it is Magellan's star, rainbird and you
have crossed ten thousand miles of open water from Japan or
China, or maybe it is arcturus you have sailed, you've just got
back down from the Alaskan tundra, wrong way papyrus in
ship of cloud,

This is memory, gold digger bird, this is scent, sage and
haunted wildcat bird, bird of salt air, and it could be any
ocean but it is this ocean, and you are cloud and cloud is ash,
and nuclear blast on the atoll is punishing and that rustle
in the bunchgrass is a soldier who never gave up and never
gave in, you are no surrender, you are american as hell, a
helicopter in the Mekong dawn, you are laysan albatross,
hatched in sand, bred on atoll, missing in action and a
midway baby in your radioactive nest, and maybe i'd say
atoll created by coral growth, or maybe i'd say seamount, and
maybe you are jungle jacket and boonie hat, or agent orange
— a steady rain hisses in your wings like chemical madness,

And, rice paddy bird populated by palm trees, you are
taro and wild boar rampaging through the crag, let off on
insufficient evidence, you are My Lai in the sandlewood, you
are napalm scrawled in the written volcanic eye, rainbird!
you have crossed my ocean too, you have returned me
to original being, you are devil of made air, fresh, fresh,

temptation incarnate, fragrant as eucalyptus, insulting as flak that cuts through the Pacific fog, suffusion of bluegill in the mangrove swamp, atmosphere in the making, seed of terrible new conquests, civilization stuck in your mighty aviator maw — it could be any ocean, rainbird, any ocean, but it is this ocean, good morning!

THIS SHADOW LIKE BLOOD BEFORE MY EYES

This shadow, this light, i am down with it, i am good with it and i will not be long, this song, this song, i am under the stars with you, clairvoyant one, i won't be long but i want you to sing it, now, now, it's a comfort to me, it eases the futility, i am an old man in his nightmare, i have the eyes of a small child gently pleading, i may offer you rust or a golden locket, o tell me of fathers ruined, of brothers murdered, tell me of the blood emptying out,

Tell me of the lost cloth of darkness with which you wrapped and wrapped around yourself, the journey is thru your eyes, i'd be lost without the telling it as you saw it, you must sing it me, o one foretold, o star of navigation, o oarlock steering my ship at night, sing of rain falling thru midnight, daylight in the hellespont, wind rinsing thru the sails like siren song, which is yours, which will always be yours,

How clouds seized your brain and placed oars in your hands, how the wind shook itself out, tell it to me in this darkness between us, which is what? life, ambition, available light, which is the black sea cleaning its wounds, which is black hair on the rockshore — blood of day, sacrifice, murder, and seduction and absolution, and yes the blind eye of the sun, tell me how you seized the flame and the flame seized you, all the men shouting, o my vision,

Tell me of the dark dawn draining out, which is the betrayal of gold and cannot be washed away, tell me about the society of gods and men, of the clashing of rocks, i want the full story, i want to be one with it, full in the belly and one with it as if with child, which is a shadow that falls like blood between all men, of the fleece and of the fleece, and the fleece, and the woman, tell me of her, how she fell to the temple floor on her knees,

How she gave herself to you, and helped you to take what did not belong to you, or to your race of men

Hero of shields, hero of ambition, empire killer — birthright of gold, children, fleece, bone, yours, yours, yours,

So romantic, i am down with it.

I TAKE THE MYSTIC BLUE TAXI TO YOU

> *'Estos días azules y este sol de infancia'*
> — Antonio Machado

Look, Antonio, I'm back in New York City, every day i wear the blues, every day I drink in this bar and play the loveable introspective fool, you taught me to do that, and I listen to the beautiful people and pass your name around like a hat, even as the fascists of the 21rst century are closing in — Antonio Machado Antonio Machado, every day I carry your name in my pocket, in my wallet, a secret poem, pensive in my sad old dying days and thinking about you at the French border, 64 years old and pensive too, Franco on the march, your last days on this earth

Lorca's dead and Manuel your brother's trapped in the Nationalist zone — and yet there are blue days in New York City too, not childhood blue, gray-blue, very gray, winter gray and a different shade of blue from yours, the peril in the world today is not the peril you faced back then but it is real, and the Generalissimo never died, and Franco's not dead, and every day I feel it, fascism on the rise and I cannot reconcile myself to the news — government of pigs, they have us on the run, the oligarchs and the silencers, they have their trolls and their torturers, they have their stooges on the way with gruesome tools

And in the barstools and buzz of artificial light, in the dead black bottles of Cuervo Gold and afternoon chatter, I hear the ruthless ones, spinning like a field of dying daisies the sad counter-revolutionary song

And do you remember the hat I wore in Barcelona in
1970, Antonio, the rain was running into my eyes and
you laughed and said do not worry, my friend, Franco
could never kill the dark mystery of the common people
— you were serene, circumspect, rich with outrage — and
yes the Spanish men were surly, and yes the Catalonians
were biding their time — and yes it was in Barcelona that
I first read your words, *there is no road, the road is made
by wandering,* and followed you like a cross, carried your
words like a pilgrim or a soldier might — to the Balearics,
to Marseille, onward by ferry to Athens and Crete, to
Arvanite villages in southern Italy — to the crooked and the
cut-throat, to enclaves and broad glamorous avenues

O Mediterranean sunlight, whitewash the white, celebrate
the blue eternal!

February 22 1939, the day you died, your legacy in your
pocket (and your elderly mother beside you, ready as you
to pass over from this world into the iron fist of the grave),
we all make our preparations and I could go on about
this forever but I'm here in New York and you are gone,
beautiful Antonio Machado, *alma de fuego,* spirit of flame
— and yes there's a lot of cold around here — therefore
Antonio, whenever my little Jesus heart, like yours, goes
out, I take the mystic blue taxi to you

A PERSIAN ROSE
Les Heures Persane, Charles Koechlin

Très calme, tres reveur, the stars are in their symmetry and
a man is in his, ivory tower and the stars flow and a man is
wide awake, even as he sleeps, a man in the sense of a waking
dream, in the sense of calligraphy, painted on turtle shell
or paper, carved in the ribbed tusks of elephants, herds of
them in dying sunlight, and a man is a waking dream with or
without pigment, brush, pen, broad tipped instrument

And I am a man, I take a stylus in my hand and press these
words into my flesh, and my flesh is soft clay and i am a
poacher on the endless plains, I am my own pastorale,
composed entirely of bone and flesh and in the idyllic mode,
song of a man who composes freely, blue as an opioid, and
this is a script of nails, a man etching heaven in a song is
easily transposed, a song released like hail from clouds, a
dragon emerging from a cave, and i am here crouched like a
persian leopard

And the crouching leopard leaps, and I am fully clawed, and
I am the black tailed gazelle falling to its knees

And I am asleep, and I am awake, and overlooking the plains
of Isfahan in an ivory tower where a man can be at peace, in
an enchanted tower, high above the leopard and the gazelle,
a man in the sky dreaming of sky, a man with a voice and a
vision, I mean a man who can sing his own shadow, shadow
song, *sotto voce,* voice of an oboe, and *les heures persanes*
fill these chambers like perfume fills the lungs (disregard the

tubercular, disregard the slow death and coughing laughter of bassoons), and a man can live forever on these plains

And in the Zagros Mountains there is a mountain pass and a trail of dust, and nomads herding numberless sheep, and life is longer than the span of a single man, a caravan, a convoy,

And Isfahan is in the eyes of the beholder, an almond-eyed maiden by a marble fountain who loves a boy, immaculate, passionate, wild with love, wild for love, in love with a boy who is in an army truck in a mountain pass, nearly a woman, already a woman, hopelessly wild, for a qualified seduction, for an epitaph, for a baptismal a wedding song an arabesque — and yes, for a rose

A Persian Rose, especially a rose grown in the gardens of a hillside palace, any rose really, purchased in the market or stolen from an apartment terrace, always there is a rose and always there are terraces, and markets, and hillside palaces, and Isfahan when the sun goes to sleep, and I am a man who remains awake and composes his songs, and night is slow and atmospheric, very slow, very dreamy, and every dream an ivory tower

THE OLIVE PICKERS

Albanian Olive Pickers, John Singer Sargent

We take our rest in cool of shade we make mute gesture to heart and circumstance we measure each branch rammed with hard fruit and beat the fruit out of the tree and let the light shine through, yes we pick and we pray, easy enough to make our pay, we make the necessary adjustments we feed the flock and the flock feeds us, providers all, provided for, we are servants, to art to family to children to lord and master whose face we have never seen except in the blinding rays of sun, whose voice we have never heard, only the bees buzzing in heat of day and hush this is a secret but ownership is thievery, sanctioned by time and government

What we are is what we own and what owns u, and we are owned by sunlight only, we serve at the pleasure of the land, not men or gods, we are sweet as a kiss, tender as hands finding their way and we take our rest among trunks and tufts of tall grass, in shadow of leaf and branch, and so what — is it so wrong to be simple! in shadow in sun hands break bread, open a big jug of wine, pass it around — o secret heart which has made us free, in the sweat and labor of summer light, a moment an eternity in the olive grove, we do not ask much, the selfish and damned and the selfless too, men equal to the moment, women equal to the men and to each other, for their own sakes

To live well is treason, to love well is rebellion, art has its own reasons and so do we

STANDING BY A PALLADIAN WINDOW SWEATING OVER PIANO KEYS

The soul of a man is like water, it floats in a flat bed, it slinks down the grassy vale (Goethe, fr *Gesang der Geister über den Wassern*)

The bow of a violin works its trade, what more might a man, particularly during the time of Metternich's great French Detente, the composers of Vienna were churning out gold threads to cover its passions and its weaknesses, and what a paradise for man, Vienna so bright (and Goethe's poems so dark, oh yes the secret demonic, this struck a chord in young Franz, born in Himmelpfortgrund, aka Strong Monastery in the Sky, by 18 he was planting his dark secrets in every little waltz, no Beethoven but competent on the piano), he additionally bore a torch for the maestro at his funeral and was Salieri's last protégé, resume enough for Count Esterhazy, and of course the countess, for whom Franz held an unnatural and suspect devotion, perhaps this is why we find him sweating in a Slovak castle in 1824, the summer after France unilaterally crossed the Pyrenees

Franz Peter Schubert son of a schoolmaster, standing by the palladian window at Zseliz Castle, sweating over the piano keys and the countess' precious daughters, waving away the rose-colored spots swirling before his eyes, and what more might a man, what more might a man, his hidden nature leaping like trout from the shallowest quintet – and yes the folk dances of southern Germany, proud and adroit as jigs of burghers and kings; and yes the lieder, burbling from the lungs of man, and yes, the innocence, innocent as Gretchen at her Spinning Wheel —

but also, dark as the Erlkonig, and quite as transfixing *(Father don't you see the Erl-King, the Erl-King with his crown and train? No my son, that is nothing but a trail of mist)*, and you can hear darkness like death from his poisoned well, smoke from the lungs of prostitutes, and you can taste the dark recesses of untoward lips

Darkness in every musical phrase and happy passage, darkness in every easy fantasia, not to mention the syphilitic sonatas, the giddiness and rush of blood to his head

Are these your rose-spotted hands, my lady, hold me I am about to die

EVERY EMBRACE A CLOUD, EVERY KISS FRESH AS FRESH WATER

Life's a bitch, life's life and death's not much better, trust me i'm an old man and i've seen both, life's here to stay and death crouches at the foot of the bed waiting its turn, life's a parole and begs you home, a word, a glance, a phrase, life's a life sentence and heaven's jail and hell is pretty much the same

And the man on the subway car staring at the headlines knows the truth of it and the woman on the subway car staring at the palms of her hands knows the truth of it

And earth is eternity and the promises and threats of gods, fake news — gods are devils, they have always had it in for us — whereas a cloud that reaches down and touches the face of a mountain, that's holy, and rain that stands in a rut and runs down farm tracks and splashes onto streetcorners, holy

And there is no saved and no savior, only pigeons, and suckers and lovers and thieves — the accusers and the accused, the forgiveness of saints — and rain falls on every rooftop and baby carriage, on the rusted chassis of every abandoned car, life yields to rain, in every parking lot and perfectly cold and lonely canyon, and even in the imperfect kiss of the sun, yielding

And i trust the man who falls in love too easily, and I trust the woman who falls in love too uneasily, I am obsessed with it all — every embrace a cloud, every kiss fresh as fresh water — because love is sown in the soil of paradise and takes root and springs into riotous life in nearer soil, and can grow anywhere — in asphalt and flower, in sea and air and armpit and hair, in crack of rock, and in the darkness too where no light goes

This light, this light, love that is unlucky as coal dust and dead canaries, love that is shoved aside or taken in whole, love that is permanent shelter or embraced for an hour

Necessary, broken love, the world is fuller for it, and men and women are blinded by the holiness of its flesh, and so what — the meat and musk and sweat of love, its full muscularity — in its mad discoveries and inspirations, in the stale bureaucracy of its work and marriages, in its laborious seductions

Love — holy light giving back even as it takes, miraculous as water sprung up from soil — love, growing and dying and remaining the same, in the headlines and in the creases of the palms of your hands — love, purified by its own light, in soil, in water, in clouds —

Mistaking everything it touches for the face of god

LETTERS FROM VINCENT
A FATAL MARRIAGE WITH THE SEA

Plain as the bump on your nose and it will remain so until apples jump back into apple trees, the North Sea holds no love for men, only reckoning, dead reckoning, the surf yellow as split pea wants nothing more than to swallow someone up, the innocent or the damned,

But like the North Sea and my mother before me I am moody too, 'churned by constant winds and inhabited by monsters,' and would as soon stand like Tacitus under black clouds than with my easel and the white wind blowing,

Let the big dunes hurl fists of sand into my eyes, one with the shellfish gatherers in their bodices of serge, holding on for dear life, one with the seabirds flying and the little white horse whinnying by the wooden cart,

One with the fisherman's flag lashing this way and that — and the ship's hull coming to, cresting in the surf, clumsy as a circus bear

NOTES: View of the Sea at Scheveningen, 1882; Henri Alphonse Esquiros' Scheveningen prose passage copied by Van Gogh prob May '77 (*Even Tacitus pictured it as being churned up by constant winds and inhabited by monsters, in the foreground it is a scummy yellow, Their dress, especially the women's, is distinctive. In the winter, they wear a bodice of serge or calico, the whinnying of the waves that run, without a bit and foaming at the mouth, about the boat's keel*)

LANDSCAPE WITH DECAYING OAK TRUNKS

In Drenthe, transfiguration is in the peat,
  Just like Ruysdael, just like Jules Dupré,
I think I have found my little kingdom of
  Melancholy, a lonely place with a little white
Path running alongside, this bog with muddy
  Boots, reach toward heaven, oak stump
Buried for a century or more, what do you
  Offer but sheer decay, some black, some
Bleached white, ghost mongrels, relics of
  The great gothic shore, Race of Titans all laid
Bare and grasping toward stranger gods
  Than Heaven, a peasant is walking past, black
Against the peasant gloom, the white sky,
  Shovel to shoulder, and yes windmills are
On the horizon but in disrepair or quite nearly
  Ruined, the gloom, the gloom, two old women
In white peasant caps on the heath, cutting
  Peat, all the variations, same sterile landscape,
Charcoal metamorphosis, new life from the pool of
  Death itself, a sweet Melancholy, a Holier light

NOTES: Landscape with Bog Oak Trunks, 1883; To Theo, Drenthe, 6-7 Oct '83 (*Just like Ruysdael, Just like Jules Dupre; a little white path ran past it all; buried for a century; black figures against the white sky; I think I may have found my little kingdom*); To Theo, Paris, 9 Sep 75 (*Pa wrote to me recently, 'melancholy does not hurt, but makes us see things with a holier eye'*)

CAFÉ TERRACE AT NIGHT

White horse coming up the
alleyway an hour ago it was
hired carriages drawn from
light to light across cobble-
stones flowergirls and the
muffled sound of Brahms or
was that my imagination the
tobacconist's lamp across the
way is definitely fading, one
by one the shutters overhead
are being snapped shut, gables
and rooftops of Arles are fading
from violet to blue to black what-
ever it was we thought was sacred
in this town has dematerialized —
this café is emptying out, I count
twelve drinkers who are not ready
to go home yet they are drowning in
yellow lantern light — how long can this go
on across the café carpet the waiter's
feet are beginning to make an old
and very familiar dragging sound

NOTES: Café terrace at night, 1888; To Willemian Van Gogh, Arles, 14 Sep '88 (*On the terrace, there are little figures of people drinking. A huge yellow lantern lights the terrace, the façade, the pavement, and even projects light over the cobblestones of the street, which takes on a violet-pink tinge. The gables of the houses on a street that leads away under the blue sky studded with stars are dark blue or violet, with a green tree.*)

ROULIN THE POSTMAN

> *Instead of painting the dull wall of a mean room,*
> *I paint the infinite*

It's a shame the people in Paris have no taste for the rough
things, weather beaten things, oxherds in straw hats, men
with hoes and heavy shoulders, *le vieux paysan* cloving
through darkness, rugged dialect, feral gaze,

Curmudgeons in old slacks living on a piece of bread,
their faces set in furrows like hard potatoes,

A pity there is not in Paris more taste for rough men in
wooden clogs, plowmen in the furnace of their work,
terrific men blazing like hot tin, drinking and smoking,
ruby cheeked men in russet sunset, or Roulin the
postman, old cleftbeard with his cap on tight,

Blue-suited Roulin, the raw dignity of his pitchfork gaze,
broad forehead, broad nose, the shape of his beard, my
only friend and drinking companion in all of Arles, sitting
in a straight back chair before green floral wallpaper,
singing the Marseillaise

NOTES: Patience Escalier, 1888; Portrait of the Postman Joseph Roulin, 1889;To Theo, Arles, 18 Aug '88 (*what a mistake that Parisians haven't acquired sufficient taste for rough thing; in the furnace of harvest time; oranges, blazing like red-hot iron; instead of painting the dull wall of the mean room, I paint the infinite; one day I saw him singing the Marseillaise*); Rosenberg, K, New York Times,1 Nov '12 (*the subject's feral gaze*)

A SYNTHESIS OF ARLESIENNES
I get the feeling we are all a little dazed

To feel deeply, to feel
subtly, this is my ambition
a nobody — an oddity
this need to paint
Madame Ginoux
Madame Ginoux
Ginoux Ginoux
a synthesis of
Arlesiennes
eyes calm
flesh green
heart like a
carved olive
elbow to table
book unread
     How to form a green whole among olive trees colored
with the solemn tones of nature
Madame Ginoux
and 2 young girls,
climbing a stepladder
among cypresses
     How to know heaven in the gleaners' hand
This rage to paint orchards
won't last forever

NOTES: L'Arlesiennes (7 variations) 1888; Women Picking Olives (1889); To Paul Gauguin, Aubers-sur-Oise, 10 Jun '90 (*It's a synthesis of an Arlésienne if you like, as syntheses of Arlésiennes are rare*); To Theo and Jo van Gogh-Bonger, Auvers-sur-Oise, 7 Jul '90, ripped up and never sent (*My impression is that as we're all a little dazed*); To Theo, Arles, 6 Nov '88 (*I have an Arlésienne at last, a figure (size 30 Canvas) slashed on in an hour, background pale lemon, the face grey, the clothes black, deep black, with unmixed Prussian blue. She is leaning on a green table and seated in an armchair of orange wood*); To Theo, Arles, 9 Apr '88 (*This rage to paint orchards won't last forever*); To Theo, St Remy, 3 Jan '90 (*coloured with more solemn tones from nature*)

RED HERRINGS
They think I'm mad 'cause I drink like them and dance
with their wives until late at night but I am not I am
just a stranger in their town up all night and out at
break of day a stranger who walks out at dawn into
the fields with easel and brush, pipe clenched tight
in his mouth and his eyes on eternity — well people
are idiots, Theo, the things they find to meddle with
and petition against, no business of mine, venomous
layabouts to a man — let them call the gendarmes
and have me hauled in like a fish — let them lock me in
the asylum and lock me out of the little yellow cottage
by the railroad station I've called mine — never mind I
squarely accept my profession among them, madman!
— because you see I have a friend with a bad reputation
— Signac, the pointillist — who comes to visit— Signac the
 violent, simple and plain, who is not afraid of my work
and will smash the lock and get me in
   and o *I am tied to earth*
       by more than earthly bonds
including gratitude for the friendship of a man like Signac
and access to my work in the little yellow cottage — and so
I have given to Signac the pointillist a picture I have made —
   still life with red herrings

NOTES: Still life with herrings, 1886; To Theo, Arles, 24 Mar '89 (*Signac was very nice and very straight and very simple when the difficulty arose of whether or not to force open the door closed by the police, who had demolished the lock… As a keepsake I gave him a still life which had exasperated the good gendarmes of the town of Arles because it depicted two smoked herrings, which are called gendarmes, as you know; Do you know that expression by a Dutch poet I am tied to the earth/With more than earthly bonds. That's what I experienced in many moments of anguish – above all – in my so-called mental illness.)*

A COMMUNE IN THE BOUCHE DE RHONE

Sometimes in life they hand you a deck of cards no matter
how many times you shuffle them each hand's worse than
the last — a loser a loser a loser — something's got to give
something's got to suffer but something's got to offer itself
eventually too, to a man of talent, to a man of patience so
Vincent confined to an asylum in St Remy fabricates two
peasant women out of thin air

And yes Millet's Gleaners and a memory of the north

Two peasant women eternally bent over, double down in their
white peak caps, digging a grave in a field of snow and for what?
At least Millet's Gleaners have something to dig for — a stalk
of wheat a wee bit of loose grain, life itself

How long have these two been at it, holding this preposterous
pose for a crackpot

Patience my dear we are confectionaries
as Flaubert phrases it *talent is long patience*
he's completely daft he's besotted he has vision
see how his brush flies now

It is 1890 it is a commune in the Bouche de Rhone Vincent's
muse lies buried in asylum sheets and pillowcases — death is
root crop, Vincent Van Gogh is digging through dead snow
himself — mad potatoes! So cruel so unspectacular what shall
we make of this thing, asylum mates?

Even the sun squatting fat and yellow on the horizon between
the rooftops and snowmad clouds cannot explain

NOTES: Two Peasant Women Digging in a Snow-Covered Field at Sunset 1890; To Theo, Arles, 22 Mar '88 (*what Flaubert's phrase might have meant, 'talent is long patience' — and originality an effort of will and intense observation*)

ILLUMINATION AND FIREWORKS
POSTPONED FOR STORMY WEATHER

the fishermen know that the sea is dangerous and the storm fearsome

A field of wheat under troubled sky, a wheatfield called mankind, what do we name this field of man, ruined corn, what do we call this loaf of bread, tumbling clouds — and all men fall to the sickle or the storm some day

The prospect goes dark, limbs get lost and orchards flood in stormy weather, but too much calm isn't good for a man, and i live and work by the day, do not condemn me, beyond the wall there are new hills rising where old hills fall

Do you remember no fireworks at the municipal baths and the Bengal Light postponed 3 times, well the Bengal Light went off eventually, nothing can stop the municipal authorities from having their way —

And the people of Arles hate me now and the gendarmes have come to put me away

But whether the people at the inn smile or take my money, whether they turn or look the other way, it's all just billiards and beer, whether the sun glows green over almond trees at dusk or if, at dawn, the light of the world goes dim, i must continue my work

I am trying not to lose my skill after all, it is difficult to
acquire a certain facility for production, i will continue
my work til the last brush falls from my hands

Look at my hands, this is Holland
Look at my hands, surrounded by
sea — this is Holland, fair weather
or foul —

The herring fishermen do not remain long
on the shore, or soon put up their oars

NOTES: Chestnut Tree In Blossom, 1890; To Theo, The Hague, 29 Sep '72 (*Illuminations postponed due to bad weather, Bengal Lights*); To Theo, The Hague, 16 May '82 (*the fishermen know that the sea is dangerous and the storm fearsome;* To Anna Van Gogh-Carbentus, Auver-sur-Oise, 14 Jul '90 (*I'm wholly absorbed in the vast expanse of wheatfields against the hills, large as a sea, delicate yellow, delicate pale green, ... I'm wholly in a mood of almost too much calm*); To Theo and Jo Van Gogh-Bonger, Auvers-sure-Oise, 24 May '90 (*it's difficult to acquire a certain facility of production, and by ceasing to work I would lose it much more quickly, more easily than it cost me in troubles to acquire it*)

105

TERRIBLY ALONE, FOREVER YOUNG
There is in most men a poet who dies young,
while the man lives on

But Sainte-Beuve was talking about Millevoye the
poet, Millevoye who loved to write about death,
not life — elegies to the young, glamorously written,
romantic and doomed, *woods that I love, farewell!*
Whereas Vincent, just 22, had fifteen more glorious
Years of poetry paint and hell ahead of him, possessed
of Sainte-Beauve's fine flower of feeling and desire,
aka madness, not one for whom life's primal dream
was likely to vanish into humdrum work or the business
of life, 37 or a hundred, a man in whom the poet will
not die is young forever

Not even a revolver shot to the heart can kill the poet
inside him — the man dies, the poet lives on — 27 July
1890, nearly dusk in the village of Auvers-sur-Oise,
northern France, Vincent Van Gogh, absorbed in an
immense plain with wheat fields that climbs up as far
as the hills, boundless as the ocean, delicate yellow,
delicate soft green, Vincent left his easel against a
haystack, went behind the wall of a nearby château
and fired a bullet into his chest —

Mad. Dying. Young and alone.

Terribly alone, forever young

NOTES: Wheat Field With Crows, 1890; To Theo, Paris, 15 Jul '75 (*St Beuve said 'There is in most men a poet who dies young, while the man lives on'*) Saint Beuve, '37 (*there exists or there has existed some fine flower of feelings, of desires, some primal dream, which soon vanishes into humdrum works and expires in the course of life's business*); The Fall of the Leaves, Millevoye, 1796 (*Woods that I love, farewell*); To Anna Van Gogh-Carbentus, Auver-sur-Oise, 14 Jul '90 (*I myself am quite absorbed in that immense plain with wheat fields up as far as the hills, boundless as the ocean*) Emile Bernard to Albert Aurier, 2 Aug '90 (*On Sunday evening he went out into the countryside near Auvers, placed his easel against a haystack and went behind the chateau and fired a revolver shot at himself*)

MISSING PORTRAIT

East of coffins, in the manner of all eyes which cannot quite read the sky, uncertain eyes set in a bold fabric of arabesques, landscapes imprinted with cornflowers and forget me nots, eyes like coiled rope, oilrags piled in a corner of the room, painting what you are told not to paint, with your hands, with your eyes, with your mouth and your beard,

The sun stands still in wheatfields, almond trees are blossoming again,

The noisy beast and storm in your head won't quit and where is that calmness you said was going to return to the world, where the smooth as sea glass, where the old currency, your hair is wax candles, *Fou-Roux*, your dead ear dumb as a ditch canal, your beard is pewter, eyebrows locked in mock ruin, your eyes blazing like two tabs of acid or butter in a frying pan,

No one is safe from you, Vincent, your gaze is crooked

Crooked as a summer pavilion for mad women to do their dancing in

IN LIFE HIS LIFE WAS BEAUTIFUL

In life his life was beautiful, as if all the attitudes and expressions of the human body were inadequate to express him, as if the human form was a small vessel for most men and existence a sea, perilous, whereas he was larger than that, immutable, though he was made from the same ultimate substance as all men, ie water; in appearance he was crafted from something of the 'other,' as if from a block of Persian marble, which made him seem in life more imminent, more dimensionally complete than the others, for which he was made lord of the others, and light of the world, for which he had eyes like a sphinx and words that could pierce heaven, like a painter pierces a canvas, like a violinist pierces the musical spheres with his bow

He was natural and without analysis beloved among peers, he was impossible to withstand, standing upright he seemed the height of a pyramid; lying down he was a wonderful lover, he took many to his side, boys, women, men, men, many lovers, his mouth was drawn from the most voluptuous doxologies, impossible, timeless, uniformly sacred and necessary, in form he was unchangeable, in form he was a crouching lion, self sufficient, self regulating, a self-acting mode of existence for which growing and growing seemed inevitable, until the high plateau of his artificial parentage spilled over and he poured out of himself

too much grace, too much grace!

And then came the race from himself, into legend — like an ur-river running to the sea, and he became, to us, all image, not the substance of a man, not an actual man, but a metaphor for a man — for example bees in a blossoming meadow, for example endless poppies in a sun drenched field

SUNSET, EASTER SUNSET
All Sunday the weeping cherry tree
threw down its long hair, doing its
innocent best in the fragrant breeze
to break my heart
   forsythia yellow, cherry
   pink, a heart that will not
   break cannot mend
bee and gardener, lion and lamb,
all grown dim and merciful in the
sweetly setting sun, and the great
spilling out of easter complete

WE ARE BIGGER THAN FLOWERS

We are bigger than flowers but the city is bigger. what is bigger than nature? money. what is more eternal than spring? greed. do breezes die in the architecture? do rivers flow underground where pavement has been laid down? you bet your rose garden they do. nature is silent before the things made by man. silent, but undefeated. the people too, undefeated if they reach out to each other. every cigarette shared on a streetcorner at is a flower. every subterranean kiss is a revolution.

Any act of love or human charity can bring the walls of a city tumbling down.

This is why a pothole is a handshake with heaven and a conspiracy against the machine. because it is beneath us to worship the machine. because we are human, and the city is a beat virgin wreathed with mist and steam and artificial light. because we shake our fists and jackhammers rattle our skin like holy bones. because we are bigger than flowers.

I am vaporous before the gods — my heart babbles down the road like a garbage truck.

EASY
How easy to admire sunsets
migrating birds and the flower
vendor wreathed in yellow light —
this city is safe from a safe distance
you said, buying yourself a longstem
rose for the long ride home, and kissed
me under the canopy — it was after midnight
the air was cold you had raindrops in your
hair the smoke of centuries wreathed us
both in a delicate envelope of rain —

You took my hand and smiled at the homeless man
balancing the world on metal crutches at the bottom of
the subway stairs

How easy it is, you said, to be a little kind
dropping a few coins into his paper cup

NOT THE KISSING KIND
My daddy used to say *i am
not the kissing kind and drinking
wine is for frenchmen* but
he was from Kansas he never
seen an ocean til he crossed
one ie the war broke out
and there he was in the European
theater a jazzed up farm boy
with a rifle in one hand and
in the other a case of penicillin
yeah he was walking across
France all right he was killing nazis
and making the world safe for
democracy again and not one of those
boys in the entire company figured
him for a woman's man until he met that
Irish girl in London he was on R&R
and anyhow didn't learn much out of
the experience, he couldn't even
kiss her properly, she kept kicking
at him like a mule the whole time,
kicking so bad she nearly got away

After the war he followed the oil rigs
and kept to himself and no one much
figured him for the marrying kind
except for mom who of course saw
something in him the others couldn't —

Life's sad like that said mom, *life's funny and sad, like
jazz, full of twists and turns, and you can't explain
nothing in this world, but particularly love.*

I COULD NEVER EXPLAIN
I could explain why i never thought of girls much but no one ever listens to me

Before you, that is
with your lips like cork
with your lips like
footprints in wet sand

AN ARMY OF MEN TO KEEP MEN OUT

Soldiers of god, our god, not yours, los cruces of gold,
blood in the desert, spilled by hand, god of protective
armor and feathered serpent, god of the wall a thousand
miles long, 20 feet high, 20 feet thick, and the border
patrol that snakes like a river of venom from man to man
and death to dust, from fear to futility, in wet season and
in dry, separating body from body, mother from child

God of the numberless poor rising up to take back their
inheritance, of the old, the penniless, the embraceable
and damned, humvee rising, indigene hunted down,
pregnant refugee lurking in the thick rooted ditch,
caught in a flash flood or searchlight beaming, the
sprung trap, the village burned, the wedding party lit up
in flames

Give us this day our daily rocket, the drone strike
that swallows straw rooftops whole and spits out our
children, tooth, nail, schoolbook and prayer, give us
this day our cookpot and cracked skull, joined in holy
matrimony, and the poplars torn limb by limb and
erected for barricades, and the flesh poured out like
poured concrete, and skin and tendon strung up and
swung by rope from trees, by the neck, by the ankles, by
the wrists by the throat —

God of a god, that made man to worship god, not man,
god brown as soil, green as corn, who protects fields
from drought and disease, cradles livestock like newborn
at the spring, who irrigates, seeds, and harvests, who
puts fallow fields to the torch

No earthly force but that which has been given us by you
No earthly force but love, unless you count the rifle barrel
No earthly force but the power to turn against each other

God who gave men to grow fertile in valleys and alongside streams, yellow with the yellow sun, bending with the breeze in spring

God who made man out of maize and gave men dominion over everything on earth, except each other, so he handed out rifles

God who taught us to say 'the streets of my heaven are lined with gold; the streets of your heaven are lined with shit'

I will kill any man who trespasses against us
I will raise me an army of men to keep men out

TRAPPED IN AMBER FATAL TO THE TOUCH

A stirring in the maelstrom, trouble in the celestial
soup — o to be Christ on the gibbet Helen on the cross a
beautiful machine an artifact of a race of men trapped in
amber fatal to the touch

To be in touch with God's touch, God's perfect engine of
the humming universe, to be on a moonlit trail, partner
to original grace conspirator to the grave

To be receptive to the elements, traveler in the lonely
storm, stormy weather itself, stormy weather could
mingle with the sky

To be one with the Earth even in its hell bent turbidity,
Earth made new Earth made pregnant with space with
hail with leaf and brimstone

The salt and seafoam of prairie intelligence itself

O to be beautiful like that, to be beautiful like anything,
a machine given to the race of men by the government of gods

Given from heaven without guilt without explication

Ticking after all this time still ticking after all this time

GIVEN WITHOUT RESERVE, TAKEN TO LIFE'S LIMIT
> *anyone who spends their life waiting*
> *for god has missed the obvious*

She flung away her bonnet, as in bone, as in blood, she stood
at the foot of the garden, as in green eyes shining, though
he arrived unannounced, a truancy, a vagrant, though he
was smoking a stogie and juggling dynamite, as in took bits
and a handle, she let him in anyway, as in instantaneously,
and became the full text of the man, reflexively, gathered the
shavings of his lathe, as in bouquet, the manner, conduct
and opinion of the man, the full condition and

Instinct of him, followed the very letter and law of his
mouth as he spoke, she grew round and timid and aware,
as in fecund, traced the shadow of his jaw, as in fence or
forecast, sat silent as a clock on a wall, as in mirror, grew
large in him like a lily in good soil, prepared to produced
in abundance, as in wheat, she rolled with his gait, trap-
like, and he sitting there with his sleeves rolled up, and he
sitting there in her daddy's leather chair, she invited him to
partake of her, and he did

> That which was not approved — that
> which ought not to have happened

By degrees, not violently, given without reserve, openly —
    taken to life's limit, mercy not offered or apology

A RAINY AFTERNOON IN NEW YORK CITY

i remove my coat
i take off my hat
i shake out my
umbrella, take
a seat at the bar
and place my dog-
eared copy of
   heart of aztlan,
  rudolfo anaya,
on the countertop
dear bartender
capitalism is a
sin and i am
transient in the
western world --
i have no nation
save you -- the
solace of hard
places and open
spaces holds no
meaning to me
there is no man
woman or child
from albuquerque
to new york city
who can make

consolation pour
from a tap like you

the human geography of all the americas cannot map
my current joy

SHADOW OF DREAMTOWN

It's all the same in the shadow of dreamtown there is no
reason to rush daylight has made its play the game was
on but now it's not the hipsters are done clipping the
wings of syntax they have drifted out of the room thank
god it's our turn now we are the long haired aliens from
the recent past we have always been here with our soft
accents and we do not care we do not make waves

This is the third way the silent path inside our heads
a muted trumpet sings Miles Davis does the hand jive
in the blue afternoon — a couple of South American
overcoats slip past I follow them in the mirror behind
the bar which is teeming with gold dust and old ghosts
— the past lives everywhere in the fixtures in the walls
in the shadow of dreamtown, the past slips through the
cracks

Outside a taxicab slows to a halt a man gets out he is tan
as a deer

What I like about this place you like about this place
which is why we like each other the smoke the beer
cheap shots of brown whiskey people who have no
names so what neon light sails across the tabletop like
migrating birds this place is quiet as heaven on a Sunday
afternoon everybody's gone to the Hamptons I guess a
woman at the bar is peeling lemons over by the juke box
a man is trying to explain some complicated matter to
some other man what's the use

The bartender shrugs his shoulders he has incurious eyes his skin is smooth as eggplant he is polishing glasses he is not an unobservant man he is scrupulous though he's seen it all and keeps his trap shut the ticktock continues irregardless irregardless — yes we have seen it all lost in the afterglow we disturb nothing it's all the same this is the shadow of dreamtown

A day a month a life slips by — a fly lands on the table, let it

WATCHFUL AS THE WILD
Daylight settling, winter settling, dusklight falling rich
and red, sweet as sloe, eyes heavy, a pinpoint job ready to
explode, waiting for the pitch dark, not enough denny's
in a cup to fill a drive of these proportions, you could
paint a still life across this country and keep going,
go right off the canvas, go on painting all the way til
tomorrow

Because the wild don't quit, yet like a small child playing
hide and seek in dusty overalls and raw dungarees,
sometimes there is a shyness about the wild, and wisdom
too, you keep your pace, i keep mine — life goes on
irregardless of what we are told and i am told a lot, i keep
my own council and my eye on the long mile

And i breach no scandal and i do no harm because
bango whango — it comes back to bite you, don't it! —
whereas on a night like this, any evening really falling
across broad waters like these, love goes down easy,
watchful as the wild, hep to distances and critical of
every face in every roadster and highbanked cloud that
plays trucks overhead

Seeding the world with gems and ice, centuries,
millennia, eternities of ice! like wild birds splashing
down, the soft moans of lovers lying bankside — and i
see your face in every headlight, flickering to life, and in
these waters, biblical, still visible at dusk, i see you rising
to surfaces and my own self rising too, by this light of
light, which is light dissipating

This water, which is glint of sun that rose in Sumeria and
Jordan and Cincinnati;

A continent passing, a future which has come and gone,
hardly a trace.

CELL DOOR OPENING

This wildness of flesh, this beacon of heaven, when i am in him and he is upon me, this open flame, this breast of rock, shoulder and stone, eyes wide, myopic as bone, this prison, as sharp and as dangerous, no warning or prayer, this penetration, this broken shale, wild and strewn and plentiful to the eye, this precipice of hill, this sinking and withering and welcoming back

This death and this thorn, a resurrection of blood and flesh, in the river like cloth, over the treetops like a cloak, and a celibate moon when the wind begins to blow, the ends of mountains, no more chains, this falling away, this yellow sun and seed tossed over and over and an even yellower field of his hair and flesh, and shorn from his body and planted like seed

This bone of fish, this crack of shell, and the winnowing wind, marrow over earth, shard over shard and collapsing crag of rock, this rude odor of him, rude, inevitable, awakening, this wildness and soil and flesh striking back at the wind, in my nostrils, on my tongue and at the convent door, hand to cradle, and tooth and press of flesh, flesh, the odor and taste of it

This fruit tree when all else fails and is wooden, when all else has come to wither, and the branches shaking, and this seed upon seed, fresh, hideous, this smell of him, this fire returning to heaven what is heaven's, burning to ash what is not, earth and everything as dust and what is flame, anyway, what is to be made of it, flesh and wind, the returning to the gods

What is torn from them, a beacon, a madness, this cell door opening

HE REMEMBERS THE SUN, THE ONLY LIGHT HE SEES
Sometimes the gods sing, sometimes the gods laugh, sometimes a man takes a drink as night gnaws deep into his bones, because frustration is dark as a sea of blood, because he cries out for the light of some inheritance that only he sees

He who possesses an entire world in the palm of his hands, he who owns the gold in his teeth and the frost in his mouth, he who grinds corn with his molars until the corn is stolen from him

No he cannot trust anyone, only the sun which goes up and down like a gypsy violin, the sun which he used to love; he was a child, how the sun would shake and dive like a river swallow racing through summer light, from daybreak to sunset, and he raced along with the sun, he was a child, free!

They are singing in the tavern, a shepherd song, they are singing on a hillside, a soldiers song, bravo bravo the revolution, bravo bravo bravo the people!

Take up your glass, little man, fill up your time, drink deep, two hands deep, you too shall make the gods sing and laugh, you too shall make companions and martyrs out of men, and strike back at the usurpers' hearts of clay, hands that shake, how they shake, and night is terrible, even now a god casts a long shadow across the table, because the gods appear when the heart of a man has turned to clay

And of course the injustice, there is always the injustice, anyone can smell it, any man who is a man can taste it and it cannot be tolerated or spit out, injustice over tabletops, injustice across valleys, injustice over the hearts of men and the astonished bodies of women

And revolution is a seamstress stitching men together, and the sound of an entire village weeping, as village upon village stands motionless and accusative in the hallway while you drink in the shadows which are not your own

And the dogs of war hungry for flesh, and the fields barren and the armies lurking, and motorcades with flags flying, and motorcycles and generals wearing sunglasses

Take to the mountains! take up your weapons! simple men, solid men! come on man, you!

He puts his hands to his face, he can feel the loose gravel of his father's grave, he can smell the feral soil which his father's father has returned to, enriched, become; this man who puts his tongue to the roof of his mouth and his mouth is dry and tastes like blood; this man whose heart is cold; a revolution is about to start, nations shake when he lights his cigar, mountains burn when he empties his glass.

Darkness at the window, and he remembers the light of the sun, the only light he sees

THE BLIND EMPTINESS OF HANDS
   and lions came down from Othrys, leaving their valleys behind

Sometimes a man is afraid to be alone
with himself, even the shepherd among
herds on an empty hillside would rather
walk hand in hand with wild beasts and
unknown angels, call down lions from
Othrys, leaving their valley behind, than
lose himself to time's passages (this, the
sweet veil of shepherd music over dew-
soaked fields; this, the jukebox weeping
louder than a whiskey bar; this, the echo
of rifles over fawn-dappled hills).

Nighttime in the city pulls the curtain down
over a man more surely than death or duty
or intoxication of work; especially for a young
man with miles to go and no companion of his
own (this, the isolation of headphones played
louder than the silence that lives behind a shut
door; this, the voice of a mountain-pipe, hill-pine
shuddering in solemn isolation; this, a mountain
nymph hiding among a wet clump of reeds).

This, a terrible voice returning from unspeakable passages.

This, an echo of children running like gunfire down a long schoolhouse corridor.

This, the blind emptiness of hands.

NO GOLDEN FLEECE WILL SAVE YOU, SAVIORS
Le monde ancien strikes again, a ritual *sparagmos*,
disfiguring the innocents, blood sacrifice on the hillside
or in the schoolhouse, it is all the same — shot in the back,
slaughtered like a ram or hiding in a broomcloset, cut off
from the others — body from body, part from part, friend
from friend and love from love, strewn for the crows and
fresh for the crop — you preach in the name of god you
preach in the name of the people, you preach in the name of
country — country country country — home, hearth, hunt,
male dominion — you preach in the name of a power that
does not reside in your cold dead hands, but in the young
hearts shaken or combed out of existence, in the young lives
lying bloodfresh in the parking lot sun

And you hold your weapons sacred as a golden fleece over
your head, stolen from a savage land and shook at the sky

But no fleece will save or succor you, saviors, you will die
miserable, not as you have lived, arrogant, influential, rich
and already dead, (yes dead, because you have always been
dead, you've been dead for centuries, dead to humanity,
dead as human sacrifice, dead even now, your hearts are
cold and your hands are dead, and it is not in your power to
ward off death with death, it is not in your power to play the
protector, innocent and religious, no not in your power to lay
low under the wind which judges you, to survive, to live to
kill again)

Because your power derives from the country of death, not life

And you will die like Jason died, rotting in his rotted hull, hiding your eyes — like Jason in his dying ship, powerless to rule even himself, struck in the head by a beam of ruin, grasping at tattered sails like lifeshreds — and you will die as you have lived, grasping at the lives of the people, wrapped in false and murderous righteousness, clothed to the last in the raimants of blood you have placed diligent as death over the eyes of our children

PROVENANCE

an august bird drowns in your eyes
   — Pablo de Rokha

Cannot a man who works with his hands find work,
cannot a woman who offers solace with her hands find
solace, cannot either find love, a man wanders hatless
in the dark in search of a day's pay, a woman sleepwalks
through hills and valleys, pride beds down wherever it
may, in fields of barley, on a skid row pallet, in the sound
of the vihuela or the arms of a stranger, like a strange
cat who makes his meows, pride disappears up alley and
into taverns and yes the brothels, door by red door
   This is the snake that hatched from the egg, this
      is the demagogue that has risen and is full in his belly
And I am sleepwalking through November, landscape of
lost love, the town where circumstance and melancholy
took place, I am taking my place among men, shoulder
to shoulder, coffeecups, countertops and the dull peeling
back of green, the false rhetoric of alcohol and suicide
and beside the park bench a pigeon is rotten with mites
and lice, a throttle of wings, the damage has been done,
and if I close my eyelids I see a flock of birds, singing in
the cornfields, taking wing and circling overhead
   This is the belt of fire that fenced us, this the book
      of the magician and his bride going out to dine
And snow will come, my friend, my friend, my lover,
and all we got is us, two hearts populated by a flock of
migrating birds, a single intelligence innocent in flight,
and all I have is my anchor of grief, what I know stays
behind in small places where hearts no longer even

collide, I am a jackrabbit burrowing in snow, a small creature in a blanket of endurance and listening to silence, to the wind, to the snow, listening for love in the obscure provenance, for the code of our secret alliance, ancient and original

    Whether it keeps me alive 'til new spring or destroys me
    I will wait for the sun which bore you aloft on solar wing

I OPEN MY EYES
Like a wound which opens up its mouth and lets love in,
I open and close my eyes;

Like the wings of a gypsy moth, dusty and gray, like the eyes of a sea bass cast up on the dock, lungs caved in, like sea-skate lying sideways and dying in salt gray, dull and slow and dying;

Like a woman in the bedroom dark, visioning her long lost perfect lover, i open my eyes and open and open them, i let darkness flow through me like floodwater;

Like shouts and curses of stevedores grappling along canals, like rope and hooks and rats, and whiskey bottles broken on the quay, like river otters at play, splashing, spitting back at the wind;

And the steamships carrying cocoa and oil to North America, and factory workers flowing through factory doors;

Like no more dredging, no more spillage or fear;

I open my eyes and close them, like the pages of a holy book, like sugar cane burning, like a falconer at the gate, the wounds of the heart, the plow and the soil;

O sweet harvest of blood, i open my eyes, loins joined with the loins of the earth

EMENESCU'S WAVES

We read by the stars, we make love by the moon, we weep when the sun comes up and when the sun goes down we break our promises and make new ones, we count our blessings and fill our socks with coins and folding money, we turn the sheets down and we dream of summer fields and children we will make together, many children, thoughtless children and brave, our own children careless as the world is careless and brave and carefree,

And everything is okay across nations and fields, and the cities are not dying, neither does the rust belt rust, and on the open plains endless waves of children are returning, children who will fulfil their promises and become stronger than us, men and women who will honor the gods and respect each other, who will commend and sacrifice and make children of their own and start again

Even as this blood of mine sheds, even as this voice of mine rises like coal dust rising, falls like snow in the mountains, settles like fossils in the deep, even as my heart waits like this soil of an hour or an eternity waits, or standing at the furnace with the men who sweat and strain and stoke the flames, i sweat and strain also, mechanically, humanly, I shed and fall, I am a civilization crumbling, I am a new world rising, there is no choice in the matter

In this cup of wine, sweet pleasures and forgetfulness; in this foundry of iron, ghetto rust

In this neon light the light of an oil lamp, my grandmother
at a cottage window, folding blankets and sewing, my
grandmother a thread unto herself, a skein of generations,
a patchwork of endurance against pain, a woman whose life
might have been extinguished childless but for some unusual
thing which occurred a generation ago and an ocean away

A woman of luck, a woman of hope and stubbornness,
strong of hip and endless carriage, impossibly strong,
who might have danced in palaces but she was of the
peasant kind, a woman who lives on in your quick eye
and the quicker steps of our own children as they walk
out with us through snowy fields and out along the open
shoreline, who walk as i walk, with my collar up, who
walk as you walk, with your arms swinging freely, and the
waves leap like waves, and fall, Emenescu's waves

And i do not taste in their rising the ocean's brine,
neither the bite of wind nor the fermentation of grain,
but sunlight on perpetual fields, courtship and death and
labor, dawn to dusk, the dappled heads of mice in hay,
the eminence of wheat piled high under the tousled sun,
baskets of apples and leather straps, horse flesh

And the singular smell of my own children, scalp and
hair and dander of my sons and daughters, hair upon
hair upon hair, a grain which is the future and meets
our own dying grain, that carries us forward like a
cartwheel fresh from the blacksmith's forge, this death
and transfiguration

There is no death at all, all is well, all is well, take my hand

FOR THIS MY HEART THE REVOLUTION

I bury the passion, i scrape the flesh, i set free the words that come out of my mouth, i go into the world, I speak in future tenses, like anger and surprise and men in huaraches, my shoulders cry, my cheeks sprout feathers, i am the monster my children and grandchildren learned to love and fear, to conjure up like wind, to cultivate their days with like fields of rice, i listen in the dark, i let their dying be, i am the cry of lightning, fermentation in the eagle's nest, in the kitchen of the world beans fall from my plate, spoons scrape a tin cup, and the children are at it again, and the sun rises, the sea falls

Sometimes the sky is very still, and i am an icon in a church that has known no name and the women sing verses to me, the children dance in a circle, this is a song which i have never heard, i say grace with the women, i pray for their children, i explore their bodies like bullet holes, pray! pray for the river, pray for the fruit which is my flesh, i have known no other body but this one, i have loved and been loved, gather around my bed and do not try to touch me, my sweat is my testimony, i am a bunkhouse in an open sky, my eyes penetrate deep into the earth like miners

Blood and semen is mine and i am a man, i pour myself out of my bed and into the pit of men i go, naturally, i have prepared myself a long time for this, 3500 hundred years is a teardrop in my eye, before there was heaven there was us, before us, a river

I prepare myself for this
For love, for death – for this
My heart the revolution

George Wallace is Writer in Residence at the Walt Whitman Birthplace, first poet laureate of Suffolk County, LI NY and author of 33 books and chapbooks of poetry, published in the US, UK, Italy, Macedonia and India. A prominent figure on the NYC poetry performance scene, he travels internationally to perform, lead writing workshops, and lecture on literary topics. A former student of W.D. Snodgrass (BA, Syracuse U) and Marvin Bell (MFA, Pacific U), he teaches writing at Pace University (NYC) and Westchester Community College, and has done research residencies at Harvard's Center for Hellenic Studies in Washington DC. He has worked as a Peace Corps Volunteer, health care administrator, community organizer, community journalist, active duty medical military officer and local historian. His work is collected at the Special Sections Collection, LI Studies Institute, Hofstra University.

CPSIA information can be obtained
at www.ICGtesting.com
Printed in the USA
LVHW110959180119
604175LV00021B/61/P